# FAITH AND TOLERATION

The 2017
J. J. Thiessen Lectures
and the
John and Margaret Friesen Lectures

FAITH AND TOLERATION

*A Reformation Debate Revisited*

C. Arnold Snyder

WIPF & STOCK · Eugene, Oregon

Wipf and Stock Publishers
199 W 8th Ave, Suite 3
Eugene, OR 97401

Faith and Toleration
A Reformation Debate Revisited
By Snyder, C. Arnold
Copyright©2018 Canadian Mennonite University Press
ISBN 13: 978-1-5326-7534-8
Publication date 11/9/2018
Previously published by Canadian Mennonite University Press, 2018

# Contents

FOREWORD ........................................................................... 9
   Karl Koop

INTRODUCTION .................................................................. 11

LECTURE ONE .................................................................... 21
   Scripture Alone, Faith Alone, Toleration Doubtful

LECTURE TWO .................................................................... 45
   "Compel them to come in": A Theology of Intolerance Examined

LECTURE THREE ................................................................. 71
   Hiding in Plain Sight: Anabaptism, Church, and State in Sixteenth-Century Switzerland

ABOUT J. J. THIESSEN ....................................................... 101

PAST J. J. THIESSEN LECTURES ......................................... 102

The 2017 J. J. Thiessen Lectures and
John and Margaret Friesen Lectures
were presented at
Canadian Mennonite University
on October 30-31, 2017.

# Foreword

In an age of rising social, political, and religious tensions, a book on faith and toleration is timely. In this volume, C. Arnold Snyder, professor emeritus of History, University of Waterloo, revisits several events and various discussions that took place during the Reformation era that revolved around the question of religious toleration. The author examines shifting perspectives among Lutheran theologians and investigates Swiss Anabaptist sources, shedding new light on the nature of Swiss Anabaptism in the latter half of the sixteenth century. Snyder reveals that by the end of the century, the Anabaptists of Switzerland were no longer running from "the world" but actively engaging those in power and courageously lobbying for religious toleration.

This is an important historical study on the subject of religious toleration that breaks new ground based on Snyder's own careful study of Swiss Anabaptist sources. It also demonstrates the author's keen interest and ability to reflect on different facets of toleration in present times.

The volume is based on lectures that were delivered at Canadian Mennonite University, October 30-31, 2017, on the 500th anniversary of the beginning of the Lutheran Reformation. The lectures were a part of the J. J. Thiessen Lecture Series and The John and Margaret Friesen Lectures in Anabaptist/Mennonite Studies.

> Karl Koop, Professor of History and Theology
> Canadian Mennonite University

# INTRODUCTION

On October 31, 1517 Martin Luther posted "Ninety-Five Theses concerning Indulgences," written in Latin, on the Castle Church door in Wittenberg. This event, which took place exactly 500 hundred years ago tomorrow (October 31, 2017), is popularly accepted as the beginning point of the Protestant Reformation, the ideas and events that, in the words of Denis Janz, "led to the disintegration of Western Christendom."[1] As it happens, the "Disputation on the Power and Efficacy of Indulgences" for which the Ninety-Five Theses were composed was not a very significant event in and of itself. But the theses were quickly translated into German, printed, circulated widely, and provoked lively discussion and reaction. In his theses Martin Luther challenged the authority of the Roman Catholic Church on the basis of the authority of Scripture. But this was just the beginning of what became a very public revolt. Luther did not stop with the issue of indulgences and soon had redefined the understanding of salvation itself and the role of the church in the saving process. By 1521, Luther's writings had been excommunicated by the pope.

The five hundredth anniversary of the beginning of the Reformation, marked by the posting of the Ninety-Five Theses, was commemorated in 2017 all across Europe and North America. A travelling Reformation history truck (or *Geschichtenmobile*) made the rounds in Europe and did a two-day stop at the Zurich

---

1 Denis R. Janz, ed., *A Reformation Reader* (Minneapolis, MN: Fortress Press, 1999), 69.

train station in January of 2017. In keeping with the ecumenical spirit of our times, there was a desire to include Anabaptist persons as part of the history of the Reformation in Zurich. I was invited to make a modest contribution as an historian of Anabaptism, and I wrote short biographies of Margret Hottinger and Konrad Winckler for the event. Both Margret and Konrad were Anabaptists from Zurich who were jailed and eventually put to death for refusing to recant their Anabaptist beliefs.

Those of us who have studied Anabaptism have had ample opportunity to ponder incidents of intolerance and coercion for reasons of faith, and to wonder at the lack of religious toleration exhibited particularly on the part of the emerging Protestant traditions. When I was asked to present lectures connecting in some way with the five hundredth anniversary of the Reformation, the topic of toleration in the Reformation came immediately to mind as a theme worth further exploration.

Of course the widespread persecution suffered by the Anabaptists raised the question of toleration, but more specifically, my recent work with Swiss Anabaptist sources revealed that, towards the end of the sixteenth century, Anabaptists in Switzerland were actively lobbying the magistrates in Zurich, Bern, Basel, and other city states for religious toleration. In arguing their case, they submitted sophisticated apologies and defenses of religious toleration, on religious grounds. We have long known that the early Swiss Anabaptists wanted to separate from "the world," and that they suffered persecution and martyrdom, but less well known is the fact that by the end of the century the Swiss Anabaptists had changed their attitude and approach. They no longer were fleeing "the world" in an unqualified way but were attempting instead to change the hearts and minds of those in power so that their religious communities could remain part of "the world" – albeit, a limited and "separated" part.

I found these Swiss Anabaptist appeals for religious toleration fascinating, not only because they represented a new mindset and approach, but also because these appeals referred back to the early writings of the Reformers to buttress their arguments. In their apologetic writings of the 1580s and 1590s the Swiss Anabaptists made particular reference to Martin Luther's pamphlet *Temporal Authority: To What Extent It Should Be Obeyed*,[2] citing it as an example of early Reformation arguments for religious freedom. This, it seemed to me, warranted further examination. Did the early reformers in fact champion religious freedom and, if so, what happened to that religious impulse?

The first two lectures originated with these questions, the first examining Luther's early writings in which he championed religious freedom from external coercion, and the second lecture following the later development among Lutheran theologians that defended, in essence, external coercion by the state in favour of the imposition of a Lutheran confession on all state subjects. A third lecture explored actual levels of coercion and toleration experienced by the Swiss Anabaptists by examining evidence from sixteenth-century Switzerland.

As I was exploring these issues in the historical sources, our lives in North America were overtaken by terrorist events, marked indelibly by images of two burning and collapsing towers on September, 2001 and more recently by expressions of white-supremacist violence and terrorist actions across a wide spectrum. It seems that our confident and relatively tolerant liberal democracies are being shaken to the core, with fundamental questions raised about what kinds of people and beliefs should be tolerated in our societies, and which, if any, should be excluded for reasons of security.

Although the histories of the Reformation and Anabaptism are many centuries removed from current events and are not comparable at all on many levels, the issue of religious freedom and toleration in general tied them together and seemed a subject worth pondering further, particularly from a Christian perspective. And that, in a nutshell, is what I

---

2 "Temporal Authority" (1523) is found in *Luther's Works* (Hereafter LW), eds. J. Pelikan and H. T. Lehmann (St. Louis: Concordia, 1955ff.), 45: 81-129.

have hoped to do in these lectures, moving back and forth across the chasm of five hundred years of history, holding out different facets of the question of toleration for reflection and consideration.

## TOLERATION

It is possible to trace the evolution of the meaning of the term "toleration" over time, as some scholars have done. Cicero's use of the term *tolerantia* dates back to 46 AD and was linked with a willingness to suffer patiently whatever fate had to offer.[3] This rather negative original meaning continues to be linked to the word in modern western languages. In Spanish, for example, the word *tolerar* means to "suffer with patience" or "to put up with." The old Spanish dictionary I inherited from my mother provides an example of the use of the word: "Mi estomago no tolera leche" says the original, that is, "My stomach cannot tolerate milk." It appears that people were lactose intolerant in Spain already more than a century ago. But the point is, toleration in its original sense was not a positive *virtue* possessed or exercised by a person or a state. It pointed to an attitude of longsuffering and patience when things weren't going particularly well. These more negative roots are present in the word also in French, English and German.

By contrast, when the word "toleration" is used today it brings to mind a different concept and package of connotations barely three hundred years old. Merriam-Webster defines "toleration" as "a government policy of permitting forms of religious belief and worship not officially established." The toleration of diverse individual religious beliefs within a single state was the ultimate political solution to a problem the Reformation had brought to a head: What to do when people feel so strongly about their hold on religious truth, that they insist on killing those who disagree with them? The Reformation split European Christendom apart and ushered in bloody religious wars, culminating in the Thirty

---

3 Astrid von Schlachta, "Toleranz (Religionsfreiheit)." www.www.mennlex.de/doku.php?id=top:toleranz, accessed June 21, 2017.

Years' War that wasn't resolved until the Peace of Westphalia in 1648. A few years later, John Locke published his famous *Letter Concerning Toleration* (1689). In that letter, Locke called for the separation of church and state and argued that since religious belief is a matter of private conviction, all religious beliefs should be tolerated equally.[4]

The term "toleration" as we use it today thus acquired strong ideological and political connotations that we associate with liberal, democratic societies and that include, but have extended beyond a narrow focus on the toleration of religious belief. The historian Robert Scribner has said it well:

> The modern idea of tolerance is essentially permissive, allowing those with different beliefs and lifestyles to live together without any civil or economic disadvantage. The notion implies neutrality of attitude, or at least an absence of positive hostility . . . that makes us indifferent to certain kinds of difference. It also transcends religious belief and encompasses, among other things, lifestyles, ethnicity, age difference and cultural otherness.[5]

Granted that Scribner is describing an ideal, always imperfectly realized in fact, his words outline the dream of a liberal, democratic, and pluralistic society in which personal differences are overlooked and individual rights and freedoms are defended. Insofar as we value a democratic society, we will value toleration understood in this broad sense of inclusiveness and acceptance of the other.[6] Insofar as we lean towards silencing dissent,

---

4 Heiko A. Oberman, "The Travail of Tolerance: Containing Chaos in Early Modern Europe," in *Tolerance and Intolerance in the European Reformation*, eds. Ole Peter Grell and Robert W. Scribner (New York: Cambridge University Press, 1996), 14-17.

5 Bob Scribner, "Preconditions of Tolerance and Intolerance in Sixteenth-century Germany," in Grell and Scribner, *Tolerance and Intolerance*, 34.

6 The modern attitude of toleration is nicely captured in the oft-repeated phrase written by Evelyn Beatrice Hall in 1906 in her book *The Friends of Voltaire*, "I disapprove of what you say, but I will defend to the death your right to say it."

imposing uniformity, and the coercion of those who vary from some majoritarian norm, we are leaving behind the tolerant, democratic ideals that have formed our liberal societies. We would then be moving towards some form of authoritarianism, in which individual beliefs, views, and opinions that do not meet with the approval of those in power are deemed unacceptable and punished accordingly. We will be returning to this point in due course.

It must be emphasized that the strong social and political connotations carried by the word "toleration" today were unknown to anyone in the sixteenth century. Very, very few people in the sixteenth century thought that any and all individuals and groups should be granted the freedom to believe and worship as they wished – which is our ideal notion of religious toleration today. Even today, it is safe to say that only a handful of anarchists might believe that there should be no restraints whatsoever on individual expressions of belief, the usual caveat being that one's beliefs should not be harmful to others in society or to society as a whole.

But "toleration" is not just a word or concept that has changed over time; the word also refers to an actual social phenomenon that has had concrete historical manifestations reaching back in time as far as we can see. There have been countless examples of people and states "putting up with" or "tolerating" those with whom they have disagreed, even though they were not familiar with the modern concept of "toleration" as a state policy of granting freedom of religion and worship to all citizens. There is the well-known instance of sixteenth-century Moravia where Anabaptists were tolerated and welcomed as resident aliens by nobility who benefitted from their labour and expertise. In our sixteenth-century explorations of toleration we will be examining historical discussions about the parameters of Christian acceptance or forbearance towards others whose faith led them to see the world differently.

When we examine the historical phenomenon of toleration in our small Reformation sample, we discover some peculiar features which we will note throughout. I would like to highlight four by way of introduction.

First, history shows that toleration is not an abstract, absolute value that anyone can possess, that applies to all situations at all times. Toleration is situational. Situations change and demand a concrete response to persons who believe differently from societal norms. The Reformation introduced one such situation, with huge consequences. The growing acceptance of Luther's Reformation ideas brought on a crisis of faith and worship and perhaps more importantly, a crisis of governance. People were making aggressively opposed faith claims, and kings, princes, and city magistrates were forced to decide how best to govern. The result was religious and political chaos that was not settled for about two centuries.

For those of us interested in the marginal reforming groups of the time, such as the Anabaptists, the question of governance has a coda: was there room in any territory for dissident groups that were not Catholic or Protestant? The question of toleration was a practical one brought on by the fact that a Protestant way of being Christian was being accepted in cities and states. How should a territory be governed given the presence within one state of persons adhering to different confessions of Christian faith that could be as varied as Roman Catholic, Lutheran, Reformed, Anabaptist, and Spiritualist? We will find that the theological answer and the political answer were not always in agreement.

In our own day, terrorist events have also forced the issue of toleration to the forefront, and concrete political decisions have to be made. In both historical times, events have decreed that indifference is no longer an option. The question of toleration at the political level, we may note, has not gone away but has simply become much more complicated, five hundred years after Luther's theses. Now we wonder: How can states be governed in the face of differing truth claims of all kinds? Is there a Christian voice that should be heard in this current debate? And what would that Christian voice say?

In the second place, historical examples demonstrate that concrete requests for toleration function within power relationships and expose those relationships. Those who have power in a society can assume tolerant or intolerant attitudes and practices toward those who have less power. In a word, those with power can include or exclude. Those who are powerless are really only suppliants. The powerless hope for and work for toleration and acceptance; the powerful decide whether or not, and to what degree, they will tolerate the powerless. History shows that when power relationships shift, views of toleration often shift as well, and very often not in the direction of greater acceptance. A well-known example comes from Martin Luther himself who, once he was speaking from a position of relative power, saw the establishment and protection of evangelical churches as more important than the toleration of individual beliefs he had appeared to champion earlier.[7] Christians pondering issues of toleration today would do well to keep questions of power in mind, evaluating their own stands from a perspective of critical suspicion.

In the third place, the limited historical examples we will examine below lead to the conclusion that toleration in the sixteenth century appeared to be put into practice in inverse proportion to the conviction that one's grasp of the truth was indubitable, exclusive, and the only allowable conviction. The general appeal of Christians in the sixteenth century – and this was especially true for theologians and professional church persons – was for toleration of their own truth and repression of any contrary understanding. The challenge for Christians today would seem to be not how to achieve indifference to faith understandings, but rather how to marry active faith with enough humility to allow different expressions of faith the right to their own claims to truth.

A further reason toleration offered itself as a topic worthy of further study is that at the time of the Reformation it was an issue argued on biblical grounds. The arguments of the day

---

[7] As Ole Peter Grell notes, "Within less than a decade Luther had moved from an outsider's position, hoping and wanting to reform the whole Church to that of an insider who sought to protect and secure the existence of the Protestant churches already established. Political considerations had forced him to modify his theology on this point." Grell, "Introduction," in Grell and Scribner, *Tolerance and Intolerance in the European Reformation*, 4-5.

were extensive and often detailed exegetical exercises defending dogma and practice of all kinds. When it came to the toleration of differing faith understandings, the writings of the time reveal positions ranging from rank intolerance to fairly unlimited toleration, all of which were ostensibly grounded on biblical arguments. As it turns out, the Anabaptists also participated in these debates, inserting their two cents' worth now and again, especially towards the end of the sixteenth century. It seemed worthwhile to explore these understandings of toleration in their original context, to better understand the biblical grounding of our faith traditions in a time before liberal democratic states were even in existence.

It goes without saying that no final word will be spoken here on this enormous topic. The hope is that these historical explorations and contemporary observations will provide an occasion for reflection and debate.

## LECTURE ONE

## SCRIPTURE ALONE, FAITH ALONE, TOLERATION DOUBTFUL

What does the Reformation have to do with our modern ideas of toleration? If modern scholarship is any measure, the answer would be "quite a lot." The discussion of toleration and Reformation is actually quite extensive and contentious, covering many decades. I would like to point to two contradictory narratives to lead our discussion to Martin Luther and the Reformation as such.

In the 1950s it was not uncommon to encounter a "Protestant triumphalist" narrative. In this view, the Protestant Reformation was the key historical step that provided the ideas leading to the establishment of tolerant liberal and democratic states.[1] The trajectory was said to go something like this: first, medieval Roman Catholic intolerance; then calls for toleration from the Christian humanists; then the decisive Reformation emphasis on individual faith, Christian liberty, the priesthood of all believers, and Luther's call for the non-coercion of consciences; and finally the culmination of this trend with John Locke's *Letter Concerning Toleration* of 1689 which provided the blueprint for the separation of church and state and the declaration of religion as a private matter.

---

1 Grell, "Introduction," in Grell and Scribner, *Tolerance and Intolerance*, 11-12.

Historians of ideas found many reasons to question the triumphalist narrative. A popular contrary interpretation following the Second World War, which witnessed the easy incorporation of the German Lutheran church into the National Socialist (Nazi) movement, depicted Martin Luther not as the midwife of democratic pluralism, but rather as the precursor to fascism, because of his support for state churches and his preaching of unquestioning obedience to princely power. If anything, this reading went, Luther's thought was "hostile to individualism and democracy,"[2] and instead prepared the German people for unquestioning obedience to Adolf Hitler.

Against this background of competing grand narratives, the tendency today is to draw much narrower and more qualified conclusions. The Reformation, it is now generally said, did not inevitably lead either to tolerant or intolerant societies; those developments depended rather on local circumstances and many other historical factors.[3] Lutheranism developed differently in Sweden, for example, than it did in Germany.[4] In other words, in spite of suggestive appearances, we can

---

[2] James D. Tracy, "Luther and the Modern State: Introduction to a Neuralgic Theme," *Luther and the Modern State in Germany*, ed. James D. Tracy (Kirksville, MO: Sixteenth Century Journal Publishers, 1986), 13. This volume contains excellent essays on the subject.

[3] Grell notes that tolerance and persecution have to be placed "firmly in the proper local, social, religious and political context. Consequently a far less homogeneous and less idealistic picture, of how tolerant European societies were during the reformation period, emerges in chronological, as well as, geographical terms." Grell, "Introduction," in Grell and Scribner, *Tolerance and Intolerance*, 11.

[4] Heinz Schilling concludes: "The political effects of confessionalization were thus bound up with the concentration of political authority in the hands of a sovereign who stood above ordinary mortals, with the formation of a bureaucracy differentiated by function, and with the development of a unified, disciplined – perhaps we should say 'tamed' – society. A comparison with other European states proves that these effects were by no means peculiar to Germany or to Lutheranism. Wherever the 'German special path' began . . . Luther did not begin it . . . " Heinz Schilling, "The Reformation and the Rise of the Early Modern State," in Tracy, *Luther and the Modern State*, 30.

trace no direct line of causation from Luther to Hitler, or from Luther to Locke for that matter.

I will make no attempt to survey this vast field of scholarship but instead will concentrate on some texts and stories that particularly illuminate the ideas about freedom of religion that were expressed in the sixteenth century, bearing in mind especially the sixteenth-century Anabaptist engagement with Reformation writers and writings on the question of religious toleration. The central question we will ask in this first lecture is this: How did a theology of salvation by faith through grace, which appears to lead to a theology supporting toleration of individual belief, become a theology that supported institutionalized intolerance carried out by a territorial state? As a second step we will look at an Anabaptist counter proposal.

## Martin Luther

It is no accident that we connect the question of religious toleration with the Reformation. The question of toleration became increasingly acute after 1517 and the posting of Luther's theses concerning indulgences. As Luther's Reformation ideas caught on, they brought on a crisis of faith, worship, and governance. Political decisions now had to be made about how best to govern, given that religious differences had begun to pull apart the social and political fabric.

It is no news to say that one of Martin Luther's central insights was to insist that salvation is exclusively the result of personal faith in Jesus Christ. In his 1519 *Meditation on Christ's Passion*,[5] Luther would write: "You cast your sins from yourself and onto Christ when you firmly believe that his wounds and sufferings are your sins, to be borne and paid for by him. . . . In his suffering Christ makes our sin known and thus destroys it, but through his resurrection he justifies us and delivers us from all sin, if we believe this."[6] Here Luther cited Paul's words written to the

---

5 Martin Luther, "A Meditation on Christ's Passion, 1519" in LW, 42: 7-14.

6 Ibid., 12-13, *passim*.

Romans, chapter 4, verse 25: "Christ died for our sin and rose for our justification." But, Luther insisted, faith that justifies and saves cannot be attained by human effort: " . . . you cannot believe, you must entreat God for faith. This . . . rests entirely in the hands of God." Saving faith is the result of God's work in human hearts; it is a free gift of grace.[7] Preaching the Word is the outward means God uses to awaken this inward faith. With these affirmations, large parts of the Roman Catholic understanding of salvation – penance, confession, absolution, prayers to the saints, purgatory, the mass as sacrifice – were challenged and cast aside.

With salvation by grace through faith at the very center of Luther's thought, it stands to reason that he would conclude, as he soon did explicitly, that God's free gift of faith occupies a protected place in all individuals, accessible to God alone, untouchable by coercion, sword, fire, or water. Some scholars have concluded that it was Luther's understanding of the personal, individual, spiritual, and inner nature of faith that led him to put forward powerful arguments for the freedom of conscience and non-coercion in matters of faith in his early Reformation writings.[8]

Of course Luther was declared a heretic. When Luther was summoned to appear at the Imperial Diet of Worms in 1521, his writings had already been condemned by the pope. In a dramatic scene, he stood at the Diet facing papal representatives and imperial officials, and then openly refused to recant. This is the famous moment when as schoolchildren we learned that Luther said "Here I stand. I can do no other." Debunking scholars have now shown that Luther did not actually say these exact words. What Luther did say was this: "I am bound by the Scriptures

---

7 See also Luther's *The Freedom of a Christian* (1520), in LW, 31: 333-377, especially 344-350 on faith and the "inner man." E.g., "since faith alone justifies, it is clear that the inner man cannot be justified, freed, or saved by any outer work or action at all." Ibid., 347.

8 Grell takes Luther's stand on non-coercion of faith as integral to his theology as a whole. He notes, "I think Luther's statement that 'the faith is free and no one can be compelled to believe' is a positive belief in freedom of conscience and as such as essential part of his theology of faith and grace." Grell, "Introduction," in Grell and Scribner, *Tolerance and Intolerance*, 5, n. 16.

*Scripture Alone, Faith Alone, Toleration Doubtful*

. . . and my conscience is captive to the Word of God. I cannot and I will not retract anything, since it is neither safe nor right to go against conscience. . . . May God help me. Amen."[9] The two central words here are "Scripture" and "conscience." Luther insisted he had to obey the understanding of Scripture that had captured his personal conscience or understanding. In later writings this would be justified by an appeal to Acts 5:29: We must obey God rather than man.

Luther's appeal to the ultimate authority of Scripture and conscience seemed to point to radical individual freedom. In the first years of the evangelical movement ordinary lay people also were encouraged to engage Scripture directly.[10] In some cases their consciences were made captive in ways Luther approved; in many other instances, individual consciences were made captive in ways Luther found repugnant and even frightening.

But Luther's words really were revolutionary because they laid a strong theological foundation for personal resistance to authority in matters of faith. In one humble example from 1530, nine years after the Diet of Worms, an Anabaptist miller named Hans, from Grüningen Switzerland, resisted being coerced into a recantation by pleading, "please do not burden my conscience, for faith is a free gift of the merciful God."[11] This example could be multiplied many, many times over, and it is no mystery who originated and popularized this argument.

Luther's open defiance at the Diet of Worms placed him in tremendous danger and made it very likely that he would soon be put to death as a heretic, as John Hus had been a century earlier. As he was riding away from Worms, the unrepentant

---

9 Cited in John Dillenberger, "Introduction," *Martin Luther. Selections from his Writings* (Garden City, NY: Anchor Books, 1961), xxiii.

10 " . . . in its initial propaganda, the ordinary lay Christian was idealised as the chief supporter of the Gospel. . . . In these years, there seemed to be no barriers to its success." R. W. Scribner, *The German Reformation* (Atlantic Highlands, NJ: Humanities Press International, 1986), 19.

11 "Und wellend mir min gewüssen nit bischweren, diewil der glaub ein freie gab erbarmenden Gottes . . . " Emil Egli, *Aktensammlung*, nr. 1635 (Jan. 9, 1530; Grüningen), 694.

Luther was subjected to a friendly "kidnapping" by soldiers in the employ of Duke Frederick of Saxony, Luther's lord and patron. Duke Frederick had Luther hidden safely away at one of his strongholds, the now-famous Wartburg castle. This got Luther out of harm's way and undoubtedly saved his life. But Luther was extremely vulnerable and could not be assured of his ultimate security, in spite of having a noble protector.

Less than two years later, Luther published a pamphlet entitled *Temporal Authority: To What Extent it Should be Obeyed*,[12] a writing that would remain a central point of reference in subsequent debates on toleration. Luther began by outlining two kingdoms coexisting in the world: the kingdom of God, and the kingdom of this world. True believers belong to the kingdom of God,[13] and need no external laws "since Christians have in their hearts the Holy Spirit, who instructs them and causes them to wrong no one, to love every one, willingly and cheerfully to suffer injustice and even death from every one."[14] The law is for the unrighteous, said Luther, which describes the vast majority of people. Luther believed that "among thousands [of people] there is scarcely a single true Christian."[15] This mass of non-Christians (or the "unrighteous") belong to the kingdom of the world and the law, and they are necessarily subject to the sword. "A wild, savage beast is fastened with chains and ropes, so that it cannot bite and tear as it would normally do," wrote Luther.[16] The worldly government is tasked with keeping social order, and it has an undeniably large job to do.[17]

---

12 "Temporal Authority: to what extent it should be obeyed," in LW 45: 81-129.

13 "Temporal Authority," 88.

14 Ibid., 89.

15 Ibid., 91.

16 Ibid., 90.

17 "For this reason God has ordained the two governments; the spiritual, by which the Holy Spirit produces Christians and righteous people under Christ; and the temporal, which restrains the un-Christian and wicked so that . . . they are obliged to keep still and to maintain an outward peace." Ibid.

*Scripture Alone, Faith Alone, Toleration Doubtful*

Still, Luther set strict limits on actions allowed by temporal authorities. Temporal rulers, Luther stated clearly, had no business whatsoever attempting to legislate matters of faith. His own words are too good not to quote: "Where the temporal authority presumes to prescribe laws for the soul," Luther wrote, "it encroaches upon God's government and only misleads souls and destroys them."[18]

That is pretty clear: there can be no valid coercion in matters of personal belief. But in 1523 Luther kept hammering this nail until he was certain it was flush.[19] In case the point had been missed, he wrote "how can a mere man see, know, judge, condemn and change hearts? That is reserved for God alone." And again, "it is futile and impossible to command or compel anyone by force to believe this or that."[20] Luther even quoted the well-known saying *Die Gedanken sind frei*: Thoughts are free; they are not subject to taxes.[21]

Luther's conclusion returned to the justification he had used when confronting his papal and imperial overlords at Worms. He wrote "How he believes or disbelieves is a matter for the conscience of each individual . . . the [temporal authority] should be content to attend to its own affairs and let men to believe this or that as they are able and willing, and constrain no one by force. For faith is a free act, to which no one can be forced."[22] Luther, faced with the possibility of Catholic compulsion of his conscience, argued in 1523 against any such coercion, noting the

---

18 "We want to make this so clear that every one will grasp it, and that our . . . princes and bishops, may see what fools they are when they seek to coerce the people with their laws and commandments into believing this or that." Ibid., 105.

19 "No one shall or can command the soul unless he is able to show it the way to heaven; but this no man can do, only God alone. Therefore in matters which concern the salvation of souls nothing but God's word shall be taught and accepted." Ibid.,106.

20 Ibid., 107.

21 Ibid., 108.

22 "Indeed, it is a work of God in the spirit, not something which outward authority should compel or create." Ibid., 108.

negative result: governments that attempt to coerce faith "compel weak consciences to lie, to deny, and to say what they do not believe in their hearts."[23] Even in the case of so-called heresy, the answer is not coercion but rather preaching the Word of God so that hearts may be changed from within.

Luther's arguments for the non-coercion of consciences spread quickly and had a long life. Out of many examples we can note a case from among the radicals who were moving towards an Anabaptist position. In 1524, a year after Luther's writing, the soon-to-become Anabaptist leader, Balthasar Hubmaier, wrote a tract titled "On Heretics and Those who burn them"[24] which closely echoed Luther's position and arguments.[25] It is a sad irony that only three years after writing this tract Balthasar Hubmaier would be tried as a heretic by Roman Catholic authorities and executed by being burned at the stake in Vienna. In 1528 the Lutheran pastor Johannes Brenz took up the topic in response to the savage execution in 1527 of the Anabaptists Michael and Margareta Sattler by Catholic lords.[26] Brenz was no fan of

---

23 Ibid., 108. "Even if their subjects were in error, it would be much easier simply to let them err than to compel them to lie and to utter what is not in their hearts . . . " Ibid., 109.

24 Balthasar Hubmaier, "On Heretics and Those who burn them" (September, 1524) in *Balthasar Hubmaier: Theologian of Anabaptism*, trans. and eds., H. Wayne Pipkin and John H. Yoder (Scottdale, PA.: Herald Press, 1989), 58-66.

25 "Secular authorities wield the physical sword; Christians wield the spiritual sword of the Word." The evidence shows that Hubmaier heeded this model as the reformer of Waldshut, limiting the power of the magistrates to coerce Anabaptist belief or practice. "The Waldshut Anabaptist community of 1525 was a believers' church of the majority, supported by political power but not extending its membership to all within the city-state – that is, the Anabaptist church in Waldshut was neither a 'state church' (on the Zurich model) nor a 'separatist minority' (a "sect")." C. Arnold Snyder, "The Birth and Evolution of Swiss Anabaptism," Mennonite Quarterly Review 80, no. 4 (October, 2006), 556. Discussion of this issue in ibid., 555-58.

26 His book was called "Whether a worldly magistrate should be allowed, in divine and common law, to condemn the Anabaptists to death through fire or sword." (*Ob ein Weltliche Obrigkeit in Göttlichen und billichen Rechten die Widertäuffer durch Fewer oder Schwerdt vom Leben zum todt richten lassen möge?* [1528]). Modern critical edition in *Werke. [Von] Johannes Brenz*, Band 1, Teil 2 "Frühschriften," eds. Martin Brecht, Gerhard Schäfer, and Frieda Wolf

*Scripture Alone, Faith Alone, Toleration Doubtful* 29

Anabaptism, which he thought was divisive and heretical, but he argued that insofar as the Anabaptists only committed spiritual sins, and did not harm the common peace, they should be tolerated and simply instructed in the true faith.[27]

It seemed that insofar as the wider context was Roman Catholic oppression, Martin Luther's arguments against coercion proved useful.[28] But the evangelical arguments soon turned against individual freedom of religion, in the favour of Protestant states enforcing "true Christian practice" on all subjects, on pain of punishment. The appeal to religious toleration, championed so strongly by Luther himself, had a very brief shelf life in the mainstream Reformation. What happened?

Even a partial answer is complex. As one part of the answer it has to be said that Luther and other early reformers, such as

---

(Tübingen: Mohr-Siebeck, 1970), 480-498. Brenz concluded that if heretics live honorably, in peace, in civil and worldly order, and don't harm others, the worldly sword has no legal right over them. Paul's words in Romans 13 call for the punishment of visible evil doers, not for the punishment of spiritual sins against God. Ibid., 483. Against the argument that Anabaptists wished to have community of goods, and that this would lead to civil disorder, Brenz countered that no one was being forced to have goods in common, and so the Anabaptists were simply making the same error as had the monks and nuns, whom no one proposed killing. Ibid., 488. Therefore the magistrates should refrain from punishing the simple Anabaptists and give them over to the spiritual arm for instruction. But the magistrates were to be vigilant in maintaining social peace and harmony, and should punish any who disturb the public peace, whether they were Anabaptists or not.

27 "Darumb sol die oberkeit yhr peinliche hand von den einfeltigen widerteuffern abwenden und sie dem evangelio zu straffen gedeyen lassen, hab aber sunst acht, das in friden und erbarer einigkeit gelebt werde. Dann wer darwider handelt, er sey tauffer oder widertauffer, der sol sein gepurende straff von yhnen empfahen." Ibid., 498.

28 Christian Scheidegger notes that besides Johannes Brenz, Andreas Osiander, and Wenzeslaus Linck of Nuremberg also opposed coercion of religious dissenters. Konrad Klauser, former pastor in Zurich and then schoolmaster in Brugg, also opposed using the sword against heretics, since Christ and the Apostles had not. He eventually was expelled from the church for stubbornly holding to that opinion. Erasmus and Sebastian Castellio also were prominent persons who opposed coercion in matters of faith. Urs B. Leu and Christian Scheidegger, eds, *Die Zürcher Täufer, 1525-1700* (Zurich: Theologischer Verlag, 2007), 87-88.

Zwingli, attributed more power to the hearing of Scripture than history would warrant.[29] Rather than promoting unity, the widespread appeal to Scripture resulted instead in a broad range of interpretations that Luther, and especially the territorial princes, found downright alarming. Luther saw his beloved Reformation taken in different directions by persons like the Zwickau Prophets, Thomas Müntzer, and Andreas Karlstadt, among others, all of them appealing to the authority of Scripture. And then late in 1524 the Peasants' Revolt broke out and brought on a crisis that Luther could not avoid.[30]

The peasants' grievances long pre-dated the Reformation, but many peasants now seized the moment and justified their social demands with direct appeals to Scripture.[31] The "Twelve Articles of the Peasants" are a case in point. The widely-circulated Articles asked that Scripture alone be used as the measure of the justice of the peasants' social demands, and the margins were filled with Scripture references, apparently providing the biblical foundation for all claims.[32] In conclusion, the offer was made to

---

29 Grell noted that Luther seems to have believed sincerely that "everyone would eventually see the light through evangelical instruction and preaching . . ." Grell, "Introduction," in Grell and Scribner, *Tolerance and Intolerance*, 6.

30 John Oyer writes, "Why did [Luther] decide [the Anabaptists] should be killed? Partly because they appeared to him as increasingly seditious, and partly because he was losing faith in the belief that the mere releasing of the Word would bring about the defeat of heresy. The Word could not do it alone." John S. Oyer, *Lutheran Reformers against Anabaptists* (The Hague: Martinus Nijhoff, 1964), 138.

31 The articles that the Klettgau peasants drew up in January 1525, appealing to "godly justice" as the only norm for a Christian society, are among the first to explicitly link grievances to the "Word of God." Tom Scott and Bob Scribner, ed. and trans., *The German Peasants' War: A History in Documents* (New Jersey: Humanities Press, 1991), 251. For a review of the historiography, see James M. Stayer, *The German Peasants' War and Anabaptist Community of Goods* (Montreal and Kingston: McGill-Queen's University Press, 1991), 19-44. "The most universal factor in the Peasants' War of 1525, which distinguished it from the long succession of localized risings before and after it, was its connection with the Reformation." Ibid., 34.

32 The widely-circulated "Twelve Articles" of the peasants, with their explicit appeal to Scripture, were composed by the end of February, 1525. Translation

*Scripture Alone, Faith Alone, Toleration Doubtful*

withdraw any articles that were incompatible with the Word of God.[33] Catholic critics warned the princes and magistrates that following Luther's call to reform by "Scripture alone" would result in social chaos.

Martin Luther reacted immediately with a pamphlet titled "An Admonition to Peace: A Reply to the Twelve Articles of the Peasants in Swabia"[34] in which he set out to clarify the right and proper way that consciences should be instructed by divine Scripture. While Luther exhorted and scolded both the princes[35] and the peasants, in the end Luther came down hardest on the peasants. Luther said that even if the rulers were wicked and tyrannous, Scripture still forbade rebellion against authority (Romans 13; 1 Peter 3; Deuteronomy 33:2: "Vengeance is mine, I will repay saith the Lord"). By rebelling, the peasants had "put [themselves] above God."[36]

It appeared from Luther's early writings that he was advocating freedom of personal conscience in spiritual matters. But now it became clear that Luther did not really hold that position. He understood the conscience to be free only when it was captive to a *proper* reading of Scripture. And Scripture properly read, as Luther clarified, established that the Gospel of salvation pertained to the inner person only, while Scripture as law established the supreme authority of government in all temporal matters. Here Luther had recourse again to the two kingdoms – the laws of

---

of "The Twelve Articles," including the Scripture references in the margins of the original text, in Scott and Scribner, *The German Peasants' War*, 252-57.

33 Ibid., 257. Luther's demand for a Reformation based on Scripture had very obviously been pressed into service by the peasants. Other peasant articles had identified Luther by name as one who should determine the justice of the peasant cause. Kyle C. Sessions, ed., *Reformation and Authority: The Meaning of the Peasant's Revolt* (Lexington, MS: D. C. Heath, 1968), 29.

34 LW, 46: 17-43.

35 It was the rulers who were the real cause of the uprising, and God's punishment would continue even if the peasants were to be defeated. Luther called the rulers to repentance and a new attitude of dealing responsibly with the peasants. Ibid., 19-23.

36 Ibid., 25-26.

the Christian are precisely what Jesus said: turn the other cheek, suffer, bear the cross. In what sounds like an Anabaptist reading, Luther pointed out that "it is not for a Christian to appeal to law, or to fight, but rather to suffer wrong and endure evil." If the peasants were in fact Christians, they would suffer wrong. But since they were rebelling against authority, "leave the name of Christian out of it," Luther counseled.[37] "Insofar as you are Christian, you will advance your cause by prayer and endurance only."[38]

Insofar as the Twelve Articles claimed to be based in Scripture, Luther dispatched one article after the other with biblical counter proofs and dismissed the relevance of the Bible passages in the margins.[39] Luther was especially upset with the third article which had argued that "there shall be no serfs, for Christ has made all men free."

He clarified that the peasant understanding of political freedom was not at all what he had meant when he had written about Christian freedom. "That is making Christian freedom a completely physical matter. Did not Abraham and other patriarchs and prophets have slaves?" This article, Luther concluded, "would make all men equal, and turn the spiritual kingdom of Christ into a worldly, external kingdom; and that is impossible. A worldly kingdom cannot exist without an inequality of persons, some being free, some imprisoned, some lords, some subjects."[40] Christians, Luther repeated, "should keep still, suffer and make their complaints to God alone."[41]

In his wholehearted defense of the need for inequality in society, Luther clarified just how far he stood in his political

---

37 LW, 28; 31-32.

38 Ibid., 32.

39 "The man who composed your articles is no godly and honest man. His marginal notes refer to many chapters of Scripture on which the articles are supposed to be based. But he talks with his mouth full of nothing, and leaves out the passages which would show his own wickedness and that of your cause." Ibid., 34-35.

40 Ibid., 39.

41 Ibid., 40.

*Scripture Alone, Faith Alone, Toleration Doubtful*

thinking from the communal principles of the peasants and, for that matter, from modern liberal and democratic ideals that would come later. Luther believed that equality happened only in the spiritual realm which was personal and invisible; social inequality, on the other hand, is the necessary social order established by God. He counseled calm and sober negotiations between the parties.[42]

This did not happen, and the Peasants' War of 1525 became a widespread unruly and bloody affair. In response Luther wrote a second tract that unfortunately appeared in print not during the conflict itself, but just after an estimated 70 thousand peasants had been slaughtered by noble armies. This notorious pamphlet was titled "Against the Robbing and Murdering Hordes of Peasants."[43] Since the peasants had not heeded the biblical advice they had requested from Luther, but instead set out to "rob and rage and act like mad dogs," Luther stated that he would now instruct the rulers how they should proceed "in these circumstances."[44] Luther's counsel to the rulers was unequivocal and harsh: "Here is a place where you can release, rescue, help. . . . Let whoever can stab, smite, slay. If you die in doing it, good for you! A more blessed death can never be yours, for you die while obeying the divine Word and commandment in Romans 13, and in loving service of your neighbor." And Luther concluded, "If anyone think this too harsh, let him remember that rebellion is intolerable."[45]

---

42 He concluded by stating that both rulers and peasants were acting against God, each in their own ways. Ibid., 40-42.

43 LW 46: 49-55.

44 Ibid., 49. The peasants, wrote Luther, had committed three grave sins: they broke their oaths of obedience to their rulers, and were thus perjurers; they began a disastrous rebellion like highwaymen and murderers; and finally "they cloak this terrible and horrible sin with the Gospel," thus becoming "blasphemers of God and slanderers of His holy name, serving the devil, under the outward appearance of the Gospel, thus earning death in body and soul ten times over." Ibid., 49-51.

45 Ibid., 54-55.

Martin Luther was, at best, an accidental and involuntary social revolutionary. He was a theologian who abhorred social disorder. At the heart of his thought was a spiritual conviction: sinners were promised salvation by faith in Christ through the grace of God, activated by the hearing of the Word of God which converted the hearts of those who were open to hearing the good news of the Gospel. The "freedom of conscience" that appeared to follow from this interior, individual understanding of faith, and which seemed to lie at the heart of his 1523 writing, did not really mean for Luther that all individuals were free to be informed by their own reading of Scripture. Rather, what Luther actually meant was that individual consciences were "free" to be captured spiritually by the Gospel of salvation. For those who were converted in the heart by the Holy Spirit, this meant that they were servants of all, as Christ had been, and made no temporal claims at all, as Christians, nor did they try to apply spiritual categories to the temporal realm. The same captivity to the Word of God meant, according to Luther, that through Scripture – primarily on the basis of Romans 13 – God had given divine authority to rulers in all temporal matters which Christians were divinely bound to obey.

It was Luther's appeal to the individual conscience where faith resides that led some historians to point to Luther as the central forerunner of modern individualist ideas of religious toleration and toleration generally, and Luther could have gone down this path. But the direction Luther took subsequently, when his spiritual reformation was threatened with social unrest, has led other historians to point to Luther as the father of blind obedience to political authority. We may say that a similar fork in the road is also faced in our democratic societies today, even though far removed from the sixteenth-century religious context.

Facing this decisive historical moment, Luther sought the full-out support of the territorial princes for his Reformation.[46]

---

[46] "Within less than a decade Luther had moved from an outsider's position, hoping and wanting to reform the whole Church to that of an insider who sought to protect and secure the existence of the Protestant churches already

For the territorial princes, embracing the Reformation offered a unique opportunity that was hard to turn down. By turning from the Roman Catholic church, they were free to seize and secularize church property. This significantly expanded their land holdings and their income at virtually no cost to themselves.[47] From Luther's perspective, princely protection for a territorial Lutheran church provided defense from Roman Catholic and imperial forces, who were set on destroying the budding Reformation. But the cost to the Reformation was considerable: the Protestant princes now appropriated not only church property and income but also took over former episcopal functions and demanded confessional obedience from their subjects. As one historian has put it, "The state regarded the religious confession of faith not as the product of individual conscience – which would have been 'Protestant' in the proper sense – but as the duty of the subject to the state."[48] And so the "formal confession of faith," to which subjects were expected to swear allegiance, now replaced the decision of individual consciences in matters of faith.

Luther's understanding of the Word of God may have been spiritually radical in matters of faith, but it remained socially and politically conservative – not to say retrograde – in temporal matters.[49] Most importantly, Luther made it clear that matters of faith remained in the heart, known only to God; the true church of believers would be invisible to the world,

---

established. Political considerations had forced him to modify his theology on this point." Ole Peter Grell, "Introduction," in Grell and Scribner, *Tolerance and Intolerance*, 4-5.

47 Karlheinz Blaschke, "The Reformation and the Rise of the Territorial State," in Tracy, *Luther and the Modern State*, 61-75.

48 Ibid., 72-3.

49 The historian Peter Blickle has observed that at the heart of Luther's social thinking stood the belief that authority was "sacrosanct, and active resistance to it was strictly and in principle denied." Peter Blickle, *Communal Reformation: The Quest for Salvation in Sixteenth-Century Germany*, trans. Thomas Dunlap (New Jersey: Humanities Press, 1992), 140-41.

again, known only to God. Nevertheless, the visible church would be subject in significant measure to political authorities.

By 1525 Luther's political situation had changed: he had moved from being a threatened heretic to being the leader of a growing territorial church movement. It is difficult not to correlate Luther's pivot on the question of toleration to the change in his own political power. The price of institutionalizing the Reformation, however, was abandoning the notion that "Christian freedom" included the freedom of individuals to believe as Scripture had informed their own consciences – which is the basic right Luther had claimed for himself. In the Protestant states, individuals were free to believe only the "true faith" that had already been defined by the theologians and imposed by the law of the land. Dissenting views were not to be tolerated, on pain of punishment.[50] The thinking seemed to be: the "true faith" has been discovered, so what is wrong with making the true faith the law of the land?

In reviewing this history, I find it almost breathtaking how quickly Protestant theologians forgot that their own churches were the result of rebellion and disobedience to duly established Roman Catholic authorities. It is stunning how quickly they assumed the posture of defenders of the only true faith in territories under Protestant control, calling on the civil authorities to suppress any dissenting expressions of faith. In this way, in spite of promising beginnings in the direction of religious toleration, Lutheran reform turned

---

50 Heinz Schilling makes the common observation that national bonds were weak in early modern states. "Rather, it was religious, that is, confessional, uniformity that at the beginning of the early modern era supplied the basis for social integration." Religion was the "functional equivalent of national sentiment" in 16th and 17th centuries. Political thinkers believed that "law and order can only be sustained when all – or almost all – subjects of a state belong to the same religion or to the same church. Religion, they thought, was the best instrument to produce the voluntary obedience of subjects to princes and to establish harmony between the different estates and social classes." Heinz Schilling, "The Reformation and the Rise of the Early Modern State," in Tracy, *Luther and the Modern State*, 24.

*Scripture Alone, Faith Alone, Toleration Doubtful* 37

instead to provide theological justification for increasingly absolutist states who demanded confessional obedience from their subjects. In the next lecture we will examine how, a few years later, one Lutheran theologian framed a theology of intolerance.

### ONE ANABAPTIST CRITIQUE

We should recognize at least one Anabaptist response to these developments. The most thorough Anabaptist engagement with Luther's arguments on toleration was the anonymous writing, now shown to have been written by Pilgram Marpeck, called the *Exposé of the Babylonian Whore*, published in Strasbourg in 1531 or 1532.[51] Although Marpeck would disagree with some of Luther's conclusions, he had read Luther closely and followed his basic outline.[52] Marpeck's primary criticism was that Luther had abandoned his own central arguments.

By 1531 and the writing of this tract, the establishment of the territorial Reformation was well underway. Marpeck noted that although Protestant reform had begun well, it had taken some wrong turns. Protestant teaching, Marpeck stated flatly, had been responsible for the Peasants' War. Luther and his followers had "persuaded the common people valiantly to defend the Word of God, all the while whitewashing that defence with Scripture." Then they had turned and counselled the peasants to obedience. And now, in 1531, Luther and his followers were urging "the

---

51 Translation of "Exposé of the Babylonian Whore and Antichrist; its mystery and abomination old and new..." in *Later Writings by Pilgram Marpeck and his Circle*, trans. and eds. Walter Klaassen, Werner Packull and John Rempel (Kitchener, ON: Pandora Press, 1999), 24-48. The scholarship that led to the demonstration of Marpeck's authorship is listed in ibid., 23. See also the analysis in Neal Blough, *Christ in our Midst. Incarnation, Church and Discipleship in the Theology of Pilgram Marpeck* (Kitchener, ON: Pandora Press, 2007), 81-99.

52 Neal Blough notes that "One almost has the feeling that Marpeck had a copy of *Von weltlicher Oberkeit* on his table when writing the *Aufdeckung*, even though he had his own understanding of Luther's doctrine of the two kingdoms." Blough, *Christ in our Midst*, 92, n. 44.

Princes, the nobility, and the cities to resist the Emperor."[53] This latter reference pointed to the recently-concluded Schmalcaldic League, a military alliance of evangelical states organized to oppose Emperor Charles V and the Catholic Princes.[54] The rebellion by evangelical states against the Emperor's rightful authority was certainly just as wrong as the peasant rebellion against princes and towns had been, Marpeck said.

Pilgram Marpeck did not agree with Luther that the spiritual and secular worlds were separated and insulated from one another. Instead he saw the spiritual kingdom filling the entire horizon for true Christians. Here Marpeck took issue with the Protestant understanding of faith and salvation. As Luther explained it, faith in Jesus Christ changed one's legal standing before God. God considered sinners righteous for Christ's sake, even though they remained unrighteous in fact. Marpeck understood faith differently.

> The knowledge and teaching of Christ is . . . a new birth from God. The heritage of flesh and blood cannot remain after the new birth has taken place; it must die and come to nothing. . . . It is not very complicated; one needs only to bend one's back, freely offer it to the cross of Christ following our Lord Christ (Luke 9:23), and faithfully bear that cross with gentleness, love and patience as God's lambs (Matt. 11 [10;16]).[55]

Coming to faith, said Marpeck, has to involve being visibly and tangibly changed as a person by the Spirit of God, in this very life and world. The cross that Christ bore was at the heart of this change. Without Christ's sacrifice, nothing would have changed in history. But Christ's cross and sacrifice was the beginning of the story of faith, not the end. Coming to faith meant becoming a righteous person by means of a spiritual rebirth, not simply being considered righteous by God because of one's belief about Christ's sacrifice.

---

53 "Exposé," 26. See Blough, *Christ in our Midst*, 89.

54 "Exposé," 45, n. 11.

55 "Exposé," 29.

*Scripture Alone, Faith Alone, Toleration Doubtful*

Likewise, Marpeck was not satisfied with Luther's conclusion that Christ's virtues of turning the other cheek and loving enemies as described in Matthew 5 were not meant as norms for Christian behaviour in the world.[56] To the contrary, Marpeck wrote, Christians "leave vengeance to God," and "Whoever teaches the contrary is an Antichrist, liar, and deceiver (1 John 4:20; 2 John)."[57] "Wherever the true Christ rules in doctrine and life, all fleshly control comes to an end," wrote Marpeck.[58]

Climbing over the divide Luther had placed between the spiritual and the temporal realms, between the Gospel of salvation and the temporal law, Marpeck said clearly "[Christ] rules in his own through his Spirit alone also in temporal matters, and distinguishes the spirit of the accusing, vengeful Elijah from the Spirit he gave his own. Through his Spirit they were born; through that Spirit they are still being born."[59] As for wielding the sword out of love of neighbour and for the neighbour's protection, Marpeck was very clear: "The Lord [does not desire] any help through which someone else is injured or hated. We are to love our enemies and not hate them (Luke 6:27), even though they assault us together or singly. . . . We may not injure anyone

---

56 Luther wrote in 1523: "In what concerns you and yours, you govern yourself by the Gospel and suffer injustice yourself as a true Christian; in what concerns others and belongs to them, you govern yourself according to love and suffer no injustice for your neighbor's sake; this the Gospel does not forbid, but rather commands in another place." Dillenberger, *Luther*, 375. And again: "the precedents for the use of the sword also are matters of freedom, and you may follow them or not, but where you see that your neighbor needs it, there love constrains you so that you must needs do what otherwise would be optional and unnecessary for you to do or to leave undone. Only do not suppose that you will grow pious or be saved thereby, as the Jews presumed to be saved by their works, but leave this to faith, which without works makes you a new creature." Ibid., 376.

57 "Exposé," 29.

58 Marpeck wrote: "Christ has this spiritual covenant with his own by means of a free, willing spirit which Christ mediated from the Father to those who have faith in him. [He accomplished this] through the obedience of the Spirit. It was not available to and could not be done by flesh and blood or its agencies, nor by the coercion of governments or subjects." "Exposé," 34.

59 "Exposé," 33.

for love of someone else or we revoke our love for the enemy and so miss the way of Christ."[60]

True Christians will, of course, come to the aid of those in need, as long as it can be done without harming someone else. Christians will follow after Christ in life and model his life in the world, by the power of His Spirit. They are openly living in the world as members of the new covenant initiated by Christ himself, ruled by Christ's Spirit and Christ himself, following the life outlined by Christ himself, namely a life ruled by love that excludes coercion.[61]

**OBSERVATIONS**

Can we jump over the chasm of five hundred years of history, clutching any valid conclusions for Christians today?

We should return to the fork in the road that Luther faced in the mid-1520s. It seemed he was forced to take one path or the other: either affirm individual freedom in matters of faith or support the "freedom" to believe what the authorities ordered subjects to believe – which of course was no freedom at all. When Luther and other Protestant theologians affirmed the latter – the "freedom" to obey the confession of faith mandated by the territorial prince – it is clear that they felt justified in doing so because they were sure they possessed the "true faith," and it was this "true faith" that was being imposed by the Protestant authorities.

When he was a teenager, my eldest son had a favourite T-shirt that proclaimed "Everyone is entitled to my opinion." I'm pretty

---

60 "Exposé," 33-4.

61 At the end of the tract, Marpeck returned explicitly to the matter of coercion in matters of faith. The central biblical text he referred to was Jesus' parable of the weeds and the wheat, Matthew 13:24-30. What to do when the weeds planted by the enemy begin to populate the wheat field planted by the lord? The owner of the wheat field says "let them grow together until the harvest," at which time the weeds can be separated from the wheat and burned in the fire without harming the wheat. Marpeck drew the conclusion: "He commands no one to condemn and kill with the sword. Virtually the whole of Matt. chapter 5 testifies that no one is to be coerced or dominated. . . . Those who do the opposite are of the world and are not Christ's." "Exposé," 41.

*Scripture Alone, Faith Alone, Toleration Doubtful* 41

sure he meant it as a joke, but it is actually a fair description of the logic operating in the sixteenth century and no joke at all in that context. All parties – Catholic, Protestant, Anabaptist – were convinced that they had grasped the full truth. Furthermore, it was a zero-sum game, because there was only one truth to be had. Those who opposed my truth had to be embracing falsehood; there was no other possible option. So everyone was entitled to my opinion. Out of this intolerance, out of this lack of spiritual and intellectual humility, grew religious wars and countless acts of barbarity and violence against people who dissented in matters of faith.

Have we progressed beyond the understanding that there is only one truth, and that it is identical with the one we possess? To put this in a Christian context, have we finally attained enough humility to admit that only God sees the full picture, that only God can see into human hearts, and more importantly, that we are not God? Can we accept that those who do not believe as we do may be as right as we are, in God's eyes? Or to push the envelope further, can we believe it is God's will that we tolerate and accept those who call God "Allah"? Or that we tolerate and love those who do not believe in a God at all? Or those who believe in seventeen-hundred gods?

Insofar as we are facing some analogous issues today, pitting toleration against intolerance, it seems fair to ask which path at the fork in the Reformation road Christians should take today. Very little historical genius is needed to see that it would be a terrible mistake to take the fork in the road that led to institutionalized intolerance, authoritarian states, and religious wars. I would suggest, rather, the road not taken by Christians as a whole.

Religious toleration became policy thanks to secular Enlightenment thinkers and governments, and for the most part was bitterly opposed by the churches. I believe that, however late, religious toleration should be reclaimed and reinstated as a central Christian virtue for our time. This follows from Luther's original insight that our salvation is by individual faith through the grace of God, brought to us by Jesus Christ, and so lies beyond human reach and coercion. The teaching of individual salvation by grace through faith should lead us naturally to the benign acceptance of the views God happens to plant in the hearts of other individuals. I believe that as Christians we should apply this insight, which is a call to utmost humility, as thoroughly as we can, both within the church and outside it, in society.

The history as I read it also suggests value in the Anabaptist understanding of faith. The fundamental question is not whether people simply believe, in some cognitive way, that Jesus died for their sins on the cross a long time ago, and so God considers them righteous and leaves them alone. A doctrine of salvation that releases us from a life-changing encounter with the living God can take the Christian faith down a devastatingly sterile road. An overly spiritualized faith makes it possible to somehow "believe" the story in our hearts while leaving untouched the seeds of arrogance and intolerance in our hearts.

I believe the Anabaptist corrective, long anticipated and continued in the contemplative Christian stream, should be heeded by Christians today. Faith indicates a relationship, in fact, a covenant with the living God; faith refers not just to a cognitive state of mind but to a living spiritual relationship and brings Jesus the Christ out of the historical shadows and into our present lives. Furthermore, the words and the life of Christ the head are the infallible guides for the lives of those who profess the Christian faith. No stronger case for toleration could be made than to focus the Christian life on developing a spiritual relationship with the living God, with Jesus Christ himself as head, teacher, and guide.

In spite of Christianity's less-than-stellar historical contribution to this question, Christians today should find deep resonances in the call for toleration, acceptance, and freedom from coercion that were articulated so well at the beginning of the Reformation. And furthermore, although it may not answer all the hard questions, beginning from the Gospel bedrock of Christ's command that we love our neighbours, and even our enemies, seems to me to be the truest point of departure for people who wish to call themselves Christians.

But of course, I freely grant you the right to disagree.

Now that I have tried to make a case for traveling down the road of toleration as the recovery of a Christian virtue, let me conclude by traveling down that road a few more steps and complicating

*Scripture Alone, Faith Alone, Toleration Doubtful*

our lives a little. The endless discussions about Romans 13 at the time of the Reformation may seem a little dated, especially in a democratic context, but we have to recognize that the passage does make a certain political sense even today. Even in democratic societies we value social order and justice. We still hope that governments will restrain evil and promote the common good. The prospect of anarchy, or a society in which any and all things are tolerated, is positively frightening.

One historian of toleration has noted, "Toleration is a quality that most members of modern liberal societies prize – until they have to put up with something truly intolerable."[62] Should a democratic society tolerate the propagation of religious views that promote hatred and violence against others, for example? A democratic society must value and protect toleration, and indeed it depends upon it, but ironically, it appears that there must be limits imposed on what can, and cannot be tolerated if a democratic society is to survive at all. But it is a dangerous and slippery slope, for at some point the scales may tip towards collective repression at the expense of individual freedom, and "toleration" itself can become the reason for intolerance. The line between individual freedom and collective responsibility is constantly under negotiation in democratic societies, and for this we must be thankful. In authoritarian societies, this negotiation has come to an end.

Of course, deciding what cases demand the curtailing of freedom is always fraught with difficulties. Should a society forbid women covering their faces in the name of the common good of secularism? Is the use of gendered pronouns an unacceptable encroachment on individuals who do not identify themselves in binary terms? If the purchase and ownership of automatic weapons is outlawed or limited, does this harm the common good? The debate continues, even as the death tolls mount. Should the voices of white supremacists, neo-Nazis and Ku Klux Klan wizards be allowed free access and free speech,

---

62 Philip Benedict, "*Un roi, une loi, deux fois*: parameters for the history of Catholic-Reformed co-existence in France, 1555-1685," in Grell and Scribner, *Tolerance and Intolerance*, 65.

or are their messages a species of hate crime, rightly subject to restrictive penalties under the law?

The borders of toleration are fluid and always under negotiation in a democratic society. But these are necessary conversations to pursue in our present day, just as it was necessary to pursue them in the sixteenth century and the centuries following. The good news is that we can still negotiate these questions in our democratic societies, even when we do not always agree with the conclusions of the majority. As Christian participants in these discussions we possess a sure baseline that can help shape our responses: the baseline of the words and the life of Christ and what he taught us about the meaning of love.

# LECTURE 2

## "COMPEL THEM TO COME IN": A THEOLOGY OF INTOLERANCE EXAMINED

Protestant theologians, both Lutheran and Reformed, soon supported their churches being absorbed administratively into their respective states. In these civil/religious unions, magistrates and princes required their subjects and citizens to attend their official churches and to swear agreement with the confessions of faith sanctioned by the state. Dissent was not tolerated on pain of punishment. How did Protestant theologians, beginning from a standpoint of Christian freedom and salvation by faith through grace, come to support state coercion, torture, and even execution in the name of "true faith"? In the case of the persecution of Anabaptists, part of the answer points to historical circumstances. The Anabaptists were not completely without blame for the increased wave of persecution that broke out.

In 1531 in Strasbourg, the former Lutheran preacher Sebastian Franck published his massive *Chronicle*, a vast critical compendium of church historical events.[1] Among many other things, the *Chronicle* contained unique descriptions of

---

[1] The version available to me was the 1536 reprint of the Strasbourg original: Sebastian Franck, *Chronica, Zeitbuch vund Geschichtsbibell von anbegyn bisz in diss gegenwertig . . .* MDxxxvi iar. . . . (Ulm, 1536). Franck's observations about the Anabaptists are found in English translation in *Sources of South German/Austrian Anabaptism*, ed. C. Arnold Snyder (Kitchener, ON: Pandora Press, 2001), 231-252 (Hereafter SSGAA).

Anabaptists, many of whom Franck had known personally. Franck was not uncritical, but he was a generally sympathetic observer. He described the beginnings of the baptizing movement and the persecution the Anabaptists endured, and described how Anabaptists of his acquaintance taught "obedience to the government in all things not contrary to God."[2] He went on,

> As many as I spoke to about it, said that they were there in order to suffer with patience for the sake of Christ, and not impatiently to fight. For the Gospel teaches [that it] will not be defended or affirmed with the fist, (as the peasants had in mind) but with suffering and dying. . . . as one can see in the examples of Christ and the apostles who called on no power to defend their matter with the fist. They criticize all who teach a warlike Christ and who would defend Christianity with the sword, saying that this has no support either in the teaching of Christ and the apostles nor of the first church. Therefore there is no need, according to my thinking, to be concerned about an uprising by them.[3]

Franck concluded that the Anabaptists were harmless and there was no reason to persecute them on the pretext of preventing blasphemy and rebellion. "God is strong enough to ward off and to punish all heresy," he concluded, echoing the early Luther.

Less than three years later, Sebastian Franck's depiction of Anabaptists as peaceful people whom no one should fear sounded naive and badly out of touch. In early 1534, militant Anabaptists under the leadership of Bernhard Rothmann, the Anabaptist prophet Jan Mathijs, and his follower Jan van Leiden managed a takeover of the city of Münster in Westphalia and established an Anabaptist city there.[4] The armed defense of the

---

2 "They increased so suddenly that the world became concerned about a revolt by them, though as I hear they were everywhere found innocent of this. But in many places they were cruelly and violently attacked, especially and firstly among the papists. They were captured, and tortured with burning, sword, fire, water, as well as with all manner of imprisonment, so that in a few years very many were killed in many places." SSGAA, 231.

3 SSGAA, 242.

4 For a balanced treatment that takes into account recent scholarship, see W. de

city began in late February, 1534 in response to a siege initiated by the prince bishop. Although many non-Anabaptist citizens had already left the city, the new regime now forced all citizens to choose between expulsion or conversion and baptism. All books that were not the Bible were confiscated and destroyed, money was seized, community of goods was proclaimed, and the city was declared to be under godly rule.[5]

Jan Mathijs, the apocalyptic prophet of the city, was convinced that Jesus would return to the city by Easter, 1534 at the latest. When the date arrived (April 4, 1534) and Jesus did not return, Jan Mathijs set out from the city armed and ready to do battle, in a desperate attempt to encourage Christ's coming. He was quickly killed by the besieging soldiers, his head paraded around the city walls on a lance.[6] The prophetic governance of the city now fell to Jan van Leiden. By the end of July, van Leiden had married the deceased prophet's widow and then instituted polygamy, eventually taking sixteen more concubines for himself, one of whom he executed for insubordination. He declared himself the new king David who would "establish justice in all the world and . . . prepare the way for the new Solomon – Christ."[7] After horrific famine and surreal goings-on in the final months, the city finally fell in a bloodbath to the besieging army in June, 1535.[8] Henceforth Anabaptism of any kind would be inexorably linked to the sixteen months of apocalyptic violence and chaos in Anabaptist Münster.

---

Bakker, M. Driedger, and J. Stayer, *Bernhard Rothmann and the Reformation in Münster*, 1530-35 (Kitchener, ON: Pandora Press, 2009). The brief summary of events is a useful overview. Ibid., 3-5.

5 A close paraphrase of Willem de Bakker's description, in de Bakker et al., *Bernhard Rothmann*, 4. For a profile of the remaining population of besieged Münster, see ibid., 157.

6 Ibid., 169.

7 Ibid., 5; "As befitting a new King David, Jan declared that he had been called to rule over the entire world to punish the unrighteous." Ibid., 175.

8 Brief summary in C. Arnold Snyder, *Anabaptist History and Theology: Revised Student Edition* (Kitchener, ON: Pandora Press, 1997), 214-221.

It was against the backdrop of Münster that in the following year, the Lutheran theologian Urbanus Rhegius composed one of the most strident calls for action against Anabaptists, namely the *Justification for the Prosecution of Anabaptists* (1536).[9] Calls to magistrates to not tolerate Anabaptists were already well underway: Zurich had decreed the death penalty in 1526, imperial law demanded the death penalty in 1528 and Luther and Melanchthon both called for the execution of Anabaptists by 1530. But Münster now became an essential reference point justifying action against any and all baptizers.[10] We will outline Rhegius's attempt to forge a biblical argument for the prosecution of Anabaptists, although we could also have chosen writings from Melanchthon, Heinrich Bullinger and others.[11] Rhegius could and did play his trump card of Münster repeatedly, but he also had a theological agenda: he had to address Martin Luther's earlier and powerful biblical arguments opposing coercion in matters of faith, which continued to circulate and find supporters.

---

9 Translation in SSGAA, 215-227.

10 See Oyer, *Lutheran Reformers*, passim. Oyer dates Luther's turn on the non-coercive punishment of heretics to July, 1524, where he argued in relation to Thomas Müntzer that "if the heretic began to use the fist . . . then the matter was no longer one for the Word alone." Ibid., 136. By 1530 Luther had written to Myconius that "the Anabaptists were not only blasphemous, but also seditious. They should be executed." 126; 137. Melanchthon also wrote to Myconius in 1530, calling for severe government action. Ibid., 154-55. Luther, unlike Melanchthon, was not well informed about Anabaptism and had limited theological engagement with them. Ibid., 132. Oyer concludes that, unlike Melanchthon, "the execution of heretics, for blasphemy or whatever other reasons, did not please Luther." Ibid., 139.

11 Oyer notes that Melanchthon "added reasons" to those he used in 1530 to advocate for the death penalty against Anabaptists. Oyer, *Lutheran Reformers*, 156. Melanchthon's most comprehensive text concerning the prosecution of Anabaptists was the *Verlegung etlicher unchristlicher Artickel welche die Widerteuffer furgeben* of April, 1536. Ibid., 169ff. In that tract he argued that Münster was the prime example of Anabaptist hypocrisy, evidence that they were the devil's workmen. Oyer calls the tract "the bitterest, most venomous tract he wrote against the sect." Ibid., 170.

## Urbanus Rhegius, *Justification for the Prosecution of Anabaptists* (1536)

At the beginning of his writing on the prosecution of Anabaptists, Rhegius laid out the question he would examine: "Should or may a Christian government in official capacity force people who err in the faith back to the right Christian faith, and, if they are disobedient, expel them because of their unbelief and their heresy, punish them in body and in goods, or what the fitting punishment should be."[12]

We need to note the limited scope of Rhegius's argument from the very start. He says he is addressing a "Christian government," but for Rhegius this phrase meant simply "a Lutheran government." If the "Christian government" in question had been Roman Catholic, for example, the heretics would have been the Lutherans themselves and Rhegius would have been furnishing arguments for his own prosecution. Notice also that Rhegius will be "examining" whether those who "err in the faith" should be forced back to the "right Christian faith." But given that for Rhegius the "right faith" is defined by the Lutheran confession, "erring in the faith" meant quite simply not agreeing with the Lutheran confession, and correcting such errors meant enforcing agreement with that confession.

When we restate Rhegius's thesis, we see how limited his examination is: What "fitting punishment" should be meted out by a Lutheran government to any who do not hew the Lutheran confessional line as defined by Lutheran theologians. The argumentative deck is stacked, the dice are loaded, and Rhegius moves on to his biblical proofs with some very important questions already answered. Of course, Roman Catholic, Reformed and Anabaptist Christians would not have agreed with Rhegius's basic premises, all for different reasons. Perhaps the most daring of his assumptions, flying directly in the face of Luther's initial assertions to the contrary, was that he could readily identify true faith apart

---

12 SSGAA, 215.

from "heresy" or "erring in the faith." This, Luther had argued strongly in 1523 when he was accused of heresy, can only be done by God who alone can see into human hearts.

Rhegius built his biblical argument first by reinterpreting, extending and systematically exaggerating the role of government as described in Romans 13:1-5.[13] This is the passage that Rhegius works and re-works at length. When reading Rhegius it is important to pay special attention to the logical connectors he uses, such as "since," or "it follows," or "therefore." Scripture, Rhegius says, demonstrates that government is of God, a servant of God for our good. *Since* this is true and it is *also true* that nothing is better for subjects than protecting them from errors in the faith and teaching them the true faith *it follows*, he says, (Rom. 13; 1 Pet. 2; Titus 3) that "secular government is bound by God's command . . . to take responsibility for the Christian religion."[14]

A reality check is in order here. Romans 13, verse 4 does assert that government is God's servant for good; however, it nowhere says that *therefore* government is to protect its subjects from errors in faith, by which Rhegius meant deviations from the Lutheran confession. This is simply Rhegius's deductive leap in the service of his predetermined conclusion. He continues to build on such questionable deductions clothed as Scripture throughout his writing. For example, he asserts that *since* governments are "servants and stewards of God, with their sword, [*therefore*] they are to execute everything to the honour of God and to the bettering of the kingdom of Christ."[15] Rhegius typically begins this sentence by referencing Romans 13 properly, but he ends the sentence with an outright howler. Nowhere in the entire New Testament can it be found to say that the function of government is to "better the kingdom of

---

13 A common approach among Lutheran apologists, as in Melanchthon. See Oyer, Lutheran Reformers, 171 and *passim*.

14 SSGAA, 215.

15 Ibid. Melanchthon argued likewise: "Civil government did not exist only for the political well-being of its subjects, but primarily for the honor and glory of God." Oyer, *Lutheran Reformers*, 174.

Christ." This conclusion is the word of Rhegius, not the Word of God.

Proceeding by such questionable logical leaps, by the end of his argument Rhegius can confidently state, as if he had demonstrated it with Scripture, that "a Christian government is to consider nothing more important than to keep the Christian religion pure with healthy teaching and to remove all which is against the service of God and against Christian faith and teaching."[16] And of course, by "pure and healthy teaching" Rhegius meant his own Lutheran teaching.

It is not difficult to see why Anabaptists would be unimpressed by such exegetical maneuvers and accuse the "learned scribes," as they called the state preachers, of twisting the plain meaning of Scripture. The *Short Simple Confession* that was circulating in Swiss Anabaptist circles around 1590 was contemptuous of such logic chopping. It called the state preachers "word mongers" who "have studied and learned their art and philosophy at the secular universities as one would any other craft."[17] Anabaptist critics were not impressed by the expert use of loaded syllogisms.

But back to Rhegius. Having established to his satisfaction that governments are ordained by God to legislate true Lutheran faith, Rhegius next faced head on Luther's earlier objections to coercion in matters of faith. Luther had argued that faith is a gift of God that works in us and cannot be forced upon anyone; that one must work against heresy only with God's Word and never with the worldly sword; that belief or unbelief is an invisible thing in the heart.[18] Rhegius's treatment of heresy is perhaps the most important of the points he makes in moving beyond Luther's early assertions.

Rhegius initially appears to agree with Martin Luther, and also maintains that heresy is an internal condition to be combatted with God's Word. But unlike the early Luther, Rhegius maintains

---

16 SSGAA, 222.

17 Snyder, *Later Writings of the Swiss Anabaptists*, 302.

18 SSGAA, 216.

that this is only a *first* step. He goes further, and appeals to an older authority:

> ... if the erring person persists in the damnable error and will not yield to the truth, then other means are required. St. Augustine calls it *compelle intrare* [Luke 14:23], namely, that one compels the erring one from error by force, not to teach him and make him confess, but to [make him] hear the truth.[19]

Rhegius maintained that governments can and should force persons to "hear the word of salvation" – namely the Lutheran word – in the hope that "God would give his grace and faith so that the listener would be converted and believe in Christ." In this way Rhegius could argue that faith remained exclusively God's work in the heart, and it was not faith as such that was being coerced; rather, it was the stubborn heretics themselves who were rightly being compelled into the church by governments to hear the truth from the state preachers, for their own good, in the hopes that by that means, God could bring them to the "true faith."[20]

Rhegius concluded that anyone who denies that governments should force heretics into church to hear the Gospel is denying God's Word, because God's Word "clearly says that the government is God's servant for good (Rom. 13)."[21] Here again Rhegius wishes readers to think that Romans 13 says more than it actually does. The verses do say that government

---

[19] SSGAA, 218. It is interesting that in 1523, Luther did not appeal to Augustine's famous interpretation of Luke 14:23, but rather cited a different saying by Augustine: "For faith is a free work, to which no one can be forced. Nay, it is a divine work, done in the Spirit, certainly not a matter which outward authority should compel or create. Hence arises the well-known saying, found also in Augustine, 'No one can or ought be constrained to believe'." "Temporal Authority," 81-129; cited from John Dillenberger, *Martin Luther. Selections from his Writings* (Garden City, NY: Anchor Books, 1961), 385.

[20] An Anabaptist tract from the late 1540s, "Why we do not attend their churches," addressed the *compelle intrare* issue directly and rejected it as a misreading of the text. See *Later Writings*, 529-30.

[21] Ibid., 217.

is God's servant for good, but nowhere in that chapter or elsewhere in the New Testament does it say, or even imply, that so-called heretics should be forced by governments to hear God's Word. That last conclusion is Rhegius's own wishful deduction, following Augustine's fanciful – not to say historically pernicious – rendering of Luke 14:23. It is manifestly false to assert that those who oppose coercing so-called heretics are thereby "denying God's Word."

But Rhegius's strongest argument, outside of citing Augustine at length, is the way that he moves "heresy" from an inward sin, known only to God, into an outward crime punishable by the temporal authorities. His argument proceeds this way.

> The worldly government has power to punish with the sword adulterers, thieves, murderers, rebels and other cases of wrongdoing. It follows that she also has the power to punish with the sword known, open heretics who teach error, who hold it and remain in it. This conclusion cannot be contradicted, for heresy is also counted among the fruits of the flesh, Gal. 5[:19ff], such as rebellion and murder which are punished by the sword. Heresy is worse and more pernicious than stealing, adultery, fornication and murder.[22]

Attempting to bolster his deductive leap extending the role of government into matters of faith, Rhegius cites Galatians 5:19 and the following verses where, we are told, the apostle Paul listed heresy as one of the fruits of the flesh, along with others such as witchcraft and drunkenness that are outward misdemeanors subject to discipline by the government. When we turn to these verses in Galatians, however, we do not find unbelief, false belief, or heresy mentioned there. Rhegius is again playing fast and loose with his Scriptural citations in pursuit of his desired conclusion.

But Rhegius still had an ace in the hole. Heresy should be punishable by governments, he continued, because heresy always leads to revolt. The prime example of this was Münster.

---

22 SSGAA, 219-220.

> Heresy also at all times produces all kinds of revolt, destruction of all good custom, disruption of government. Thus it is with these Anabaptist characters. Through them the devil seeks to destroy all doctrine, discipline and authority, first with hypocrisy under the appearance of God's Word, and then with open mischief. This the horrible example of the miserable city of Münster shows only too clearly.[23]

Here Rhegius laid down his trump card: the Anabaptist heresy in particular is not a matter of a secret mistaken belief in the heart, known only to God, but rather it is a visible heresy that will necessarily produce Münster-like results if the baptizers are not quickly restrained by the sword of government.[24] Rhegius then expanded on the example of Münster to argue (on the basis of Deuteronomy and other Old Testament Scriptures) that false prophets and "all evildoers" should be punished and even put to death by Christian governments as they had been in the Old Testament – as long as such punishment is done "in love" as the New Testament requires. His point that heresy "has brought with it revolt and murder" was highlighted by the lurid and frightening events in Westphalia.[25]

Münster provided the graphic example requiring governments to act against the evil baptizers, not to restrain hidden heresy as such, but to maintain outward order in

---

23 SSGAA, 219.

24 Melanchthon was already making this allegation in 1530. According to John Oyer, "Melanchthon believed that even if in individual cases the situation did not warrant severity of punishment, the government must use a strong arm because the times were dangerous – i.e., an insurrection similar to the Peasants' Revolt could all too easily reoccur." Melanchthon was writing in February, 1530 to Myconius. Oyer, *Lutheran Reformers*, 155; 154, n. 5.

25 According to Rhegius, in addition to their false beliefs, the Anabaptists also do other wicked deeds, being disobedient to the worldly government ordained by God. They consider lawful oaths as wrong, and they destroy the divine order of matrimony. They are all secret enemies of all government which they oppose in action when and where they may. They want to have all goods in common without the consent of others. And the rest of what the evil spirit perpetrates through these blinded people is now evident. SSGAA, 220.

society.[26] With the horrifying example of Münster at hand, Rhegius didn't have to argue long and hard to make his point that the baptizing heresy should be punished by temporal governments exactly as other outward and visible crimes are punished.[27]

Lost in the smoke of the Münster argument was the smoothing over of what is known to God alone and what is a punishable crime. Non-Münsterite Anabaptists agreed entirely that those who broke civil laws deserved civil punishment, be they baptizers or not; but Rhegius was making the case that baptizing adults on confession of faith – a disagreement over biblical interpretation, much like differences in understanding the Lord's Supper and the sacrifice of the mass – should be treated as if a civil crime already had been committed. This presupposed that Rhegius already knew the full nature of "true faith" and so could confidently step in and condemn "false belief" as a crime, recommending civil punishment for non-Lutheran teaching.

In the end Rhegius concluded that he had demonstrated "with divine Scripture of the Old and the New Testaments, with scriptural, well-based arguments and examples from Israelite rule and also with examples from the ancient church" that "a Christian government may properly and justly punish the stubborn unrepentant heretics and the originators and adherents of false doctrine with the sword even as it deals with other crimes. This needs to be done where Christian love, true teaching and admonition do not avail."[28] Malignant members,

---

26 "If heresy remained a secret in the heart, it could be judged by no one else but God. . . . If, however, it breaks out and eats about it like a cancer . . . then the government must punish the unrepentant heretics not with less but with greater severity than other evildoers, robbers, murderers, thieves, adulterers and such." SSGAA, 221.

27 Rhegius concluded: "If at Münster they had not watched Bernhard Rothmann so long, they might have saved the situation. Since, however, they let matters go and spared the seducer, the terrible distress followed which Germany will never forget but which will be a warning to her." Ibid., 222.

28 SSGAA, 226-27.

i.e., any who will not come to the Lutheran confession, need to be amputated lest they infect the entire body.

The Münster episode was a major disaster for Anabaptists everywhere, but it was a disaster created in part by a group of Anabaptists in the grip of apocalyptic expectation. Rhegius would have opposed Anabaptism in any case, but his arguments were aided and abetted by historical events. Münster led to the widespread expulsion of Anabaptists from Moravia in 1535, where many thousands had found toleration and refuge with Moravian lords, and Anabaptists elsewhere also faced increased repression. The long-term consequences were severe, since all baptizers were now tarred with the Münsterite brush and were forced further underground. It was almost impossible for this persecuted, underground church to refute the common charge that although they might appear pious and devout on the outside, all baptizers were inherently dangerous and seditious, plotting to launch their Münster-like conspiracy when they were strong enough.

## THE SERVETUS AFFAIR AND THE COUNTER-RESPONSE

Less than twenty years after the Münster disaster, on October 27, 1553, the learned theologian and scientist Michael Servetus was executed for heresy by the Reformed government in Geneva. He was charged with denying the Trinity and denying the legitimacy of infant baptism. John Calvin himself judged Servetus to be a blasphemer of God's honour, had him arrested, and called for his death by beheading; the magistrates of Geneva chose instead to burn him and his books at the stake. Calvin, unlike Luther, had no doubts about putting heretics to death. Heresy was an affront to God's honour, he believed, and such an affront automatically deserved death.[29]

---

29 See Roland Bainton, *Concerning Heretics. Whether they are to be persecuted and how they are to be treated. A collection of the opinions of learned men both ancient and modern* (New York: Columbia University Press, 1935; Octagon Books, 1965), 68-73. Bainton notes that "If Calvin ever wrote anything in favor of religious liberty it was a typographical error." Ibid., 74.

Voltaire noted two centuries later that the execution of Servetus was the first "religious murder" committed by the Reformation, a repudiation of the basic Protestant idea that "everyone shall have the right of interpretation."[30] Voltaire was scandalized by Calvin, and overstated the point. In fact, freedom of biblical interpretation had been abandoned in Protestant churches long before 1553, as any student of Anabaptism can tell you. Freedom of interpretation became impossible when Protestant churches became exclusive territorial churches who demanded that all subjects submit to their confession of faith on pain of civil punishment. The murder of Servetus in Geneva was just a logical extension of a theology married to territorial political power which demanded religious uniformity.

The burning of Servetus galvanized radical sentiment far and wide. It brought into focus not simply the question of religious toleration, but the broader question of what role should be played by the state or a state church synod in matters of faith. Opposition now emerged particularly from among spiritualists, Schwenckfelders, anti-trinitarians, and Anabaptists, but also from others who simply were scandalized by Calvin's actions.[31]

Nikolaus Zurkinden, Bern's city clerk who was on good terms with Calvin and certainly no radical, wrote Calvin a letter in 1554 in which he recalled his own experience and misgivings about killing people simply for their beliefs.

> I was witness to how an eighty-year-old elderly woman and her daughter, the mother of six children, were led to their deaths for no other reason than that they . . . renounced infant baptism. This was the only danger they posed, for certainly there was no reason to fear that two little ladies [*zwei Weiblein*] would lay

---

30 Stefan Zweig, *The Right to Heresy*, accessed from https://www.gospeltruth.net/zweig/heresy_chap6.htm.

31 Bainton compiles a long list of Protestants and others, many of whom followed Erasmus' lead in opposing capital punishment in matters of faith: Caspar Hedio, Conrad Pellikan, Coelius Secundus Curio, Otto Brunfels, Sebastian Franck, Jerome Gantner, Minus Celsus, and Katherine Zell, to mention a few. See Bainton, *Concerning Heretics*, 79-116.

waste to our territory with their false teaching. This one example suffices out of many possible ones. It horrifies me.[32]

Calvin's call for Servetus's death raised the spectre of a Protestant Inquisition, torturing and executing people simply because they held beliefs not deemed correct by Protestant theologians. Numerous responses supporting religious toleration now began circulating in manuscript and in print.[33]

An eloquent extended argument for religious toleration came from the pen of Sebastian Castellio a year after Servetus's burning at the stake. Castellio had been a colleague of Calvin's in Geneva, for a time, but had just assumed a post teaching Greek at the University of Basel. His tract of 1554, *Concerning Heretics. Whether they are to be persecuted and how they are to be treated*,[34] collected old arguments and marshalled new ones that prefigure views on religious toleration that would not prevail until the Enlightenment more than two hundred years later. Much of Castellio's tract would be extensively paraphrased and copied into the succeeding century. By the 1590s parts of his tract appear to have been used as a template by some Swiss Anabaptists in their pleas for toleration.

Castellio's tract was notable for the way it unmasked the central presumption at the heart of a theology of intolerance.[35] What exactly is heresy? he asked. The term cannot be found

---

32 Citation in Rudolf Dellsperger, "Die Täuferdisputation von 1538 im Rahmen der Bernischen Reformationsgeschichte," in "*'Lebenn nach der Ler Jhesu . . . ' 'Das sind aber Wir!' Berner täufer und Prädikanten im Gespräch* (Bern: Verlag Stämpfli, 1989), 79. Translation mine.

33 David Joris wrote anonymously against coercion of conscience as did Lelio Socini, both in 1553. Camillo Renato composed the *Carmen* in Traona [south of Chiavenna], in September, 1554, in commemoration of the burning of Servetus the year before. It was an all-out indictment of Calvin. George Hunston Williams, *Radical Reform*, 3rd edition (Kirksville, MO: Sixteenth Century Publishers, 1992), 874-75.

34 English translation in Bainton, *Concerning Heretics.*

35 The following owes much to Stefan Zweig, *The Right to Heresy* (1936), chapter 6, "Manifesto on Behalf of Toleration." Accessed from https://www.gospeltruth.net/zweig/heresy_chap6.htm.

in the Bible. Christians began calling one another heretics only after they had established churches and confessions. On analysis, the term heretic turns out to have no fixed content, its meaning determined by the one who uses it. Castellio concluded: "When I reflect on what a heretic really is, I can find no other criterion than that we are all heretics in the eyes of those who do not share our views."[36] But in fact, no human being can claim absolute, God-like certainty. In light of this, the Christian attitude should be one of toleration for the beliefs of others. To quote Castellio again, "We can live together peacefully only when we control our intolerance. Even though there will always be differences of opinion from time to time, we can at any rate come to general understandings, can love one another, and can enter the bonds of peace, until the day when we attain unity of faith."[37]

In challenging the claims to absolute certainty, and pointing to the limitations of human knowledge, Castellio was far ahead of his time. And of course his challenge to absolute truth claims was declared heretical.

In the 1580s and 1590s, Swiss Anabaptists began responding to the religious coercion being supported by theologies of intolerance. The recently-published *Later Writings of the Swiss Anabaptists* contains several of these appeals.[38] Although these later Swiss Anabaptists obviously found Castellio's selection of anti-coercion citations by Reforming theologians useful, they did not follow Castellio's lead in challenging claims to absolute truth. That was because the Anabaptists believed *they* were the ones who had found the truth! They were convinced that their own reading of Scripture was the correct interpretation. And in their understanding of Scripture, Christians do not coerce others. We only have time to outline the Anabaptist approach in broad strokes.

---

36 Cited in Zweig, *The Right to Heresy*. See Bainton, *Concerning Heretics*, 129: "we regard those as heretics with whom we disagree."

37 Ibid.

38 Snyder, *Later Writings*.

Needless to say, it became standard Anabaptist practice after 1535 to disavow any connection to the Münsterite horror.[39] In the petition submitted to the Basel council in 1589, the author was identified only as a believer in the Gospel "whom people call Anabaptists" (*die man taüffer nenett*).[40] The petition pointed to a group of persecuting, blood-thirsty people – meaning the Reformed preachers – who continued to spread lies about the Anabaptists, calling them rebellious and disobedient subjects. To the contrary, the author protested, the Anabaptists were loyal citizens, ready to do all that could be proven with Scripture. It was unfair to lump all the baptizers in with the Münsterites; rather, by the fruits one can recognize the tree. And so it went. Denials of connection to, or agreement with the Münsterites were regular features of Anabaptist defenses after 1535.[41]

As might be expected, the verses in Romans 13 were a frequent subject of discussion and interpretation. Anabaptist apologists underlined their readiness for obedience to the magistrates in accordance with Romans 13, always with the qualifying phrase "in all things not contrary to Scripture." Andreas Gut's apology to the Zurich magistrates in 1589 is typical. He wrote: "So we confess . . . that we owe the authorities taxes and levies, customs and tolls and all external duties. But in all matters that have to do with the faith, we

---

[39] In a plea for toleration directed to the Bernese magistrates in 1585, the writers noted: "We have and desire to have nothing to do, either in part or in general, with those in error, be they Münsterites or others, who are not grounded in the Word of God and the Holy Gospel, or to participate in their faith. Therefore our faith should not be called a misguided sect . . . " "Letter to the Magistrates in Bern," *Later Writings of the Swiss Anabaptists*, 144-45.

[40] Hanspeter Jecker, *Ketzer-Rebellen-Heiligen: Das Basler Täufertum von 1580-1700* (Liestal: Verlag des Kantons Basel-Landschaft, 1998), 133.

[41] Speaking of the state preachers, the "Simple Confession" of 1590 says "in their writings they mix us in with the false sects such as the Münsterites, among others, who in the guise of evangelical truth and Christian community had their wives in common, just like the fallen and apostate Nicolaitans, serving the abominable, impure, dissolute vice of adultery and immorality. We desire no fellowship here or there with the likes of either group, any more than the holy apostles desired to have fellowship with those false apostles who had posed as genuine and true apostles." *Later Writings*, 244.

*"Compel them to come in"*

confess that we are to look only to our teacher Christ, and learn from him."[42]

Anabaptist apologists invariably embraced Luther's early reading of Romans 13 as a text that limited the power of the magistracy to temporal matters of punishing evil and rewarding good. The "Simple Confession" of 1590 even cited Luther's own words to cement the point. Luther had written in 1523: "Likewise, where [Paul] says, 'Rulers are not a terror to good conduct, but to bad,' [Rom. 13:3] he limits the magistrates, saying that their authority does not extend over faith or God's Word, but rather that they are to rule over evil deeds."[43]

These were Luther's own words, and Anabaptist apologists now happily quoted them against later state-church theologians such as Rhegius, clarifying that they were guilty of no temporal evil deeds of the Münsterite kind. Other Anabaptist writings circulating in the 1580s and 90s likewise followed the examples of Franck and Castellio and cherry-picked anti-coercion passages from the early reformers to bolster their appeals for toleration in matters of faith.[44] In a pamphlet of 1590 explaining why Anabaptists did not attend state churches there is a section of selective verbatim copying from Luther, Melanchthon, Bucer, Capito, and even Zwingli, in which passages these early reformers supported freedom of conscience and faith.[45]

Occasionally these writings repeated the point made already by Castellio and others to the effect that in the early years, when Luther himself was being persecuted, he saw the truth clearly enough, but his successors, now hungry for political and economic power, had abandoned that early truth. Castellio had noted that if contemporary evangelical theologians had changed their minds when they were "elevated to riches and power" we should rather "adhere to their first opinion, because it was written

---

42 "Supplication to the Zurich Magistrates," *Later Writings*, 539.

43 Cited in "Simple Confession," *Later Writings*, 288.

44 See especially "Concerning Separation," *Later Writings*, 446-531.

45 This section of verbatim copying of early evangelical theologians runs from *Later Writings*, 468-475.

in a time of tribulation when men are the more accustomed to write the truth."[46] Castellio knew very well that Luther's "first opinion" had opposed coercion of consciences.

Andreas Gut's appeal to Christ as the only legitimate spiritual teacher highlighted a problem for Anabaptists in Switzerland and elsewhere: the Anabaptists pledged to be obedient to governments, but what was to be done when civil mandates commanded subjects to act in ways contrary to their simple reading of the words of Christ? In 1585 the magistrates in Bern published a harsh mandate that required oaths of obedience to the state, attendance in the state church, baptism of infants, and avoidance of any Anabaptists or their meetings.[47]

An Anabaptist response to this mandate was soon presented, anonymously, to the magistrates. According to this writing, the conflict for the Anabaptists was simply the result of a commitment to follow after Christ: "We desire from our hearts to be taught by [Christ Jesus]. . . . [We desire to] live according to [God's Word] through God's grace and power, and [according to] all institutions, commandments, and example of Christ and his Apostles, in baptism, the ban, the Supper and in all things that they have given and taught us. Therefore, we do not wish to accept anything that is taught or practiced otherwise."[48]

The commandments of Christ and the examples and practices of the apostles seemed clear to these Anabaptists, and as followers of Christ they felt called to obedience. At the same time, they also maintained their desire to be obedient to the magistrates in all laws and commandments not contrary to God.[49] And there

---

46 Castellio, *De haereticis*, translated in Bainton, *Concerning Heretics*, 127.

47 In the words of Bruce Gordon, the mandate "required all people to take the oath of obedience to the state, to attend church on Sundays, to bring their newborn child to church for baptism within eight to fourteen days, to attend the Lord's Supper, and to avoid all Anabaptist meetings." Bruce Gordon, *The Swiss Reformation* (Manchester: Manchester University Press, 2002), 210. See *Later Writings*, 141.

48 "Letter to the Magistrates in Bern," *Later Writings*, 144.

49 " . . . insofar as our loving God gives us grace, and insofar as we can obey the same without damage to our consciences." Ibid., 145.

was the rub, as these Anabaptists summarized it: "your mandate and the mandate of Christ (namely the New Testament), which is sealed with his innocent blood, contradict each other in their intention. In our simplicity, we cannot comprehend how they agree."[50]

The first cited example of this contradiction in the apology to the magistrates in Bern was not baptism, or the oath, or any other obvious "Anabaptist" issue, but rather was the matter of coercion itself and how it did not conform to Christ's words and actions.

> With us you call on the same Christ we do. Nowhere in his teaching and his life, nor in the entire Gospel do we find that we should coerce someone else. For Christ said, Matthew 5 [:43-44]: You have heard that it was said, you shall love your neighbour and hate your enemy. But I say to you, love your enemy, bless those who curse you, do good to those who hate you, pray for those who harm and persecute you, etc. Just before that he says: You should not oppose evil [Matthew 5:39]. . . . For what Christ taught us, he lived out for us in his own life, and asked us to follow him. This we earnestly wish to do.[51]

These Anabaptist apologists recognized that there were other interpretations of Christ's words in Matthew. But they confessed that for their part, reading Christ's words in anything other than their plain sense made them incomprehensible. And so they concluded, "we beg you, dear lords, do not force us against our consciences in matters of faith. For the Gospel does not allow bringing any one to faith by force."[52]

Here is a plea from Christians who sincerely desired to live as Jesus commanded, according to their "simple" reading of Scripture. As other observers noted, such a Christ-centered request could hardly be considered heretical, "un-Christian," or a threat to the political order, particularly since those requesting

---

50 Ibid., 145.

51 "Letter to the Magistrates in Bern," *Later Writings*, 145; 146, *passim*.

52 Ibid., 146.

permission to follow Jesus' words disavowed political revolt and were model citizens in other respects as well.

Of course, at the heart of the disagreement between Anabaptists and Protestants was disagreement over how to read and interpret Scripture and then how to put that interpretation into practice. The particular beliefs and practices that marked Anabaptism were routinely defended scripturally, again and again, in their writings. The "Simple Confession" that was circulating around 1590 covered thirteen central Anabaptist topics and ran to a mind-numbing 366 manuscript pages.[53] Opponents always stated that the Anabaptists had been sufficiently "defeated" in scriptural debates;[54] the Anabaptists never accepted that they had been properly heard or understood and returned again and again to their basic scriptural foundations.[55]

The Bernese authorities were not convinced by this Anabaptist apology of 1585 and continued their policy of trying to convince, expel or obliterate those who, because they had resolved to try to live lives in accordance with Jesus's words, commands, and example in the New Testament found themselves needing to disobey a civil mandate that ordered them to believe and live otherwise.[56]

---

53 See *Later Writings*, 153ff.

54 In 1589, in reply to a "supplication" written by the Anabaptist Andreas Gut, the head of the Zurich church, Johann Rudolf Stumpf sketched notes in reply. Among them is the typical observation: "That they are stubborn in standing over and against all reports, dialogues and disputations in which they have been amply and sufficiently heard. . . . Together with the wide-ranging and copious answers and refutations of the entire enthusiasms of their manifold errors and sect." *Later Writings*, 543-44.

55 The appeal for toleration sent to the Bernese magistrates in 1585 thought it necessary to at least present a cursory defense of "our other articles of the faith, baptism, ban, Supper, and other ordinances." "Letter to the Magistrates in Bern," *Later Writings*, 150ff.

56 The refusal of Anabaptists to participate in the state churches was cited as a prime example of their sedition and destruction of social unity. This argument was made early and often by Heinrich Bullinger, the staunchest opponent the Anabaptists faced. Bullinger understood the Swiss Anabaptists very well, having been present as a young man at the first debates on baptism in Zurich in 1525. From the start he classified the baptizers as theologically misguided "sec-

What we see in the Anabaptist confrontation with the state church is the opposition of two contrasting ecclesiologies. The one was externally established and administered by the state and its mandates. This state church theoretically encompassed all subjects of the state, since all were legally required to be members of that church; the visible church, then, contained a mixture of those who believed and those who did not. True Christian members were invisible and known to God alone. The Anabaptist understanding of the church, by contrast, held that it was established by the spiritual rebirth of all its members, who covenanted to join the body of Christ on earth with their water baptism, a testimony to their inner faith. This church of the reborn was not invisible but would be made outwardly visible as the Spirit made itself manifest in new lives.

These contrasting ecclesiologies go back to different understandings about the workings of faith, as noted previously. Against the Protestant teaching of salvation by faith alone, these later Anabaptists emphasized, explicitly, that "Faith alone is not enough for salvation without the power, anointing, and working of the Holy Spirit."[57] The reason that the evangelicals had resorted to the magistrates in promoting and defending their churches, says an Anabaptist pamphlet

---

tarians," that is, subverters of both political and religious unity and therefore seditious threats to the peace of the land. See Leu and Scheidegger, *Zürcher Täufer*, 98. In his 1531 anti-Anabaptist work, *Von dem unverschampten Fräfel*, for example, Bullinger hammers home the point at every opportunity that the Anabaptists are destroyers of Christian unity.

57 "Concerning Separation," *Later Writings*, 483. Good works must be visible but are dependent on a "living faith" and spiritual love. "Now outward good works belong to Christians or the church, works such as love, mercy, baptism, the ban, discipline, teaching, breaking of bread and all of the Gospel: external teaching and life belongs to the soul. Christ also promised mercy, the soul's blessing and salvation for such outer works, Matthew 25[:31-46]. That is, as mentioned above, if they flow from a living faith, penetrated by the fire of pure, godly love, without which all external works are in vain, no matter how good and glowing they appear to be, Matthew 7, 1 Corinthians 13. But now you have arranged for the secular authority to rule over the external works and to give laws to the souls in these things. You have placed the external teaching and life above the Gospel."

circulating in 1590, is that they do not have the spiritual power to be able to evangelize without such temporal support.[58] The apostles, by contrast, needed only the power of the Spirit to convert the world.[59]

And so the Anabaptist argument comes full circle, back to Romans 13 and the civil laws governing the state church.

> Guided by your rabbis and masters of lofty intellects, you make the Holy Gospel into a municipal and city law, to be obeyed just like any other outer law and worldly authority. . . . In this way you remove and mislead the magistrates out of their proper office and function . . . and you install them in the holy place which is the church, the house and temple of God, and give them authority over spiritual things, against your earlier teaching, and against the Holy Gospel, Matthew 24[:15]; cf. Daniel 11[:31].[60]

The Anabaptist critique concluded that it was the evangelical preachers, or as it calls them, the "masters of lofty intellects" who are at fault here for having crafted a false theology of intolerance with which to serve their own interests of securing power and property. The magistrates are warned against heeding such self-serving teaching, admonished not to bloody their own hands by serving as hangmen of the innocent at the instigation of the theologians.

---

[58] "Since they proceed . . . and set out to protect, uphold, and defend the teaching of Christ and the Gospel by means other than the sword of the Spirit, which is the word of God, and teach and counsel that it should be protected and defended (physically), they testify with this that they lack the sword of the Spirit." Ibid., 493.

[59] "Your understanding is that it is not possible to proceed and maintain (the outward things of the church) through the Word of God. With this you insult the power and activity of the almighty Word of God and the Holy Spirit, and also give witness to the fact that you do not have the use of the spiritual power and sword. It was with this spiritual power that the apostles, and especially the apostle Paul, converted all of the unknowing, blind, unbelieving nations, and maintained and expanded the flock of Christ without the help, action, or support of human or worldly power." Ibid., 483.

[60] Ibid., 489.

## Conclusion

I would return again to the fork in the road that Luther faced in the mid-1520s. Theoretically, he could have taken either the path that affirmed individual freedom in matters of faith, or negated individual freedom and supported the "freedom" to believe what the authorities ordered subjects to believe – which of course was no freedom at all. Urbanus Rhegius, along with other Lutheran theologians, developed Protestant theology in the state church direction, widening the reach of temporal authority by expanding the scope of Romans 13 and applying the circular logic that results when one assumes that one is in possession of the only truth.

I found a stunningly clear example of the circular reasoning behind the authoritarian position in a document from Zurich, dated 1589. In that year the head of the Zurich church, Johann Rudolf Stumpf, sketched out a reply and refutation of the Anabaptist argument (the logic of which was borrowed from Luther) that one shouldn't coerce the faith of the Anabaptists because faith is a free gift of God. Against this argument, Stumpf sketched the following notes:

> a) Anabaptism is not a true daughter of faith, therefore it is not a gift of God.
> b) For us it is the opposite: [we have] the true faith, [and] since it is a free gift of God, [it] may not and should not be coerced.
> c) But this does not mean that false faith should not be opposed and punished.[61]

Once you are convinced that you own the truth, the logic is quite simple. We have the true faith, the free gift of God, and you don't. Therefore we must defend our freedom to believe against your lack of faith, for the well being of all. Or as Stumpf says,

---

[61] *Later Writings*, 547. Stumpf was repeating the logic first laid out by Heinrich Bullinger, who argued that Anabaptism was a sect, and so arguments concerning faith did not apply to them. See "Bullinger, Heinrich," *Mennonite Encyclopedia*, I, 467-68.

"One coerces, ties up and locks up lions, bears, wolves [and] enraged people in order to keep the sheep safe."[62] But of course, this cannot be condemned as an attempt to coerce true faith because, by definition, only my church has the true faith and yours does not. When "my church" is linked to the territorial magisterial authority, the logical political conclusion appears to be some version of the doctrine of the divine right of rulers/ kings which, historically speaking, proved to be a political and theological dead end.

Sebastian Castellio, on the other hand, took the other road first sketched by Luther. He embraced and rehabilitated Luther's initial insight, safeguarding individual freedom in matters of faith, an idea pointing to the individualism eventually embraced by Locke and other Enlightenment thinkers. This led to the proposal of a definitive separation of church and state, and made possible the liberal democratic states of the modern era. Where do the Anabaptist defenses of freedom of conscience fit in this roughly-sketched history?

Harold Bender once argued that the Anabaptists were "prophets before their time," advocating liberal democratic values already in the sixteenth century.[63] It is true that Anabaptists were won over by Luther's early argument that the church should suffer no interference from secular authorities, and although this might look something like the modern notion of the separation of church and state, this political idea was never proposed or imagined by the Anabaptists. They applied the principle of "no temporal interference" to their own church only, and excluded the state from interfering in their church, but there is no evidence that they ever imagined a state that might be indifferent to religion.

---

62 *Later Writings*, 547.

63 "The Anabaptists were the only Reformation group consistently advocating religious liberty, separation of church and state, freedom of the individual conscience, and toleration of divergence in religious matters . . . " *Mennonite Encyclopedia* IV, "Religious Liberty," 292, written by H. S. Bender; see also H. S. Bender, "The Anabaptists and Religious Liberty in the Sixteenth Century," *Mennonite Quarterly Review* 29, no. 2 (April 1955), 83-100.

*"Compel them to come in"*

In our present day the key question concerning toleration asks how much toleration one is willing to extend to those who disagree with one's point of view. This "toleration of divergence in religious matters," which Bender attributed to the Anabaptists, was really not their concern. In fact, history demonstrates that the Anabaptists and their descendants were not very good at tolerating divergence in religious matters even within their own groups. At the heart of Anabaptist thinking was the conviction that they were being true to the biblical instructions that established the true church. That is, they believed they were establishing the *only* true church. Very little "toleration of divergence" would be seen in the Anabaptist churches themselves, let alone in relation to other professions of faith.

If it goes too far to claim Luther as the father of liberal democratic ideals, it also goes too far to claim the same for the Anabaptists. Along with their state-church contemporaries, the Anabaptists also were certain that contrary views had to be false; they were as much children of their own time as were their state-church contemporaries. Anabaptist exclusivity limited the reach of their concept of toleration.[64] As victims of persecution by the powerful, they could and did plead that toleration be granted to them to believe and worship as "resident aliens," or as "conforming nonconformists." Still, they freely excommunicated dissidents from their churches. Granted, they did not kill them, and certainly this was an advance for their age. But the Anabaptists were not imagining states or churches that would somehow value all truth claims equally.[65] Here contemporary

---

64 Hans J. Hillerbrand, *Die Politische Ethik des Oberdeutschen Täufertums*, (Leiden: E. J. Brill, 1960), 21. See the entire section "Täufertum und Glaubensfreiheit," 20-23 for relevant observations.

65 There were a few exceptions among the more spiritually oriented Anabaptists. In Hans Denck's commentary on Micah, he wrote "das auch je einer den andern, er sei Türk oder heyd glaub was er wöll, sicher wirt lassen ziehen unnd wohen, durch und inn seim landt . . . Es soll keyner den andern, daz einer eyn heyd, ein jud, oder Christ were, lassen entgelten sunder durch alle landt eim jeglichen im namen seines Gots vergunnen zuo ziehen." Cited in Hillerbrand, *Politische Ethik*, 22. Kilian Auerbacher wrote to Martin Bucer, "Ich wais auch das nymer mer recht ist einen im glauben zu nöttigen, er glaub wie er woll, es

spiritualist thinkers such as Hans Denck, Sebastian Franck and Sebastian Castellio cast the net of forbearance wider, and so better anticipate modern attitudes of toleration.

In conclusion, let me pose one challenge to Anabaptist descendants now living in the twenty-first century: To what extent do our churches today embrace the principle that it is only God who sees into human hearts? And given that this is true, and given the concrete example of Jesus, do we therefore conclude that our churches should be as inclusive as they can possibly can be? The question of toleration, and its reach and application in the church and in society, has not gone away, but has only become more acute as the centuries have passed.

---

sey Jud oder Turck, auch so ainer nicht rechtgeschaffen glaubt noch glauben woll." Cited in ibid.

# LECTURE 3

# HIDING IN PLAIN SIGHT: ANABAPTISM, CHURCH, AND STATE IN SIXTEENTH-CENTURY SWITZERLAND

It is common knowledge that the Anabaptist movement was born in Zurich, in Felix Mantz's mother's house near the cathedral, on or around January 21, 1525. And we also know very well that the baptizing movement spread quickly to the surrounding Swiss countryside and cities, soon reaching Basel, Bern, Schaffhausen, Solothurn, St. Gallen and Appenzell. Likewise it is a familiar story to recount Zwingli's opposition to the baptizing movement and the Zurich government's growing legislation against it. By April 1526, Zurich had passed a law decreeing death by drowning for anyone failing to desist from baptizing activities. In January 1527, Felix Mantz became the first Anabaptist martyred by Zurich, drowned in the Limmat river. After this, the baptizing movement went underground, and we would be hard pressed to tell any stories about it. Nevertheless, there are stories to tell. It's just that they are buried in archives and hard to access.

Anabaptism was outlawed in all the Protestant and Catholic states of the Swiss Confederation. How did Anabaptists manage to survive in Switzerland over the course of the sixteenth century, as they in fact did? It is a fascinating story of resistance to assimilation and the exercise of sporadic toleration in the face of pressures to coerce obedience.¹ But first, a bit of context.

Ulrich Zwingli set the basic direction for reformation in Swiss territories. In some of his early writings Zwingli, like Luther, argued that governments had no power to legislate church matters or matters of faith and conscience. Nevertheless, Zwingli's fundamental vision of reform was less individualistic than was Luther's. For Zwingli, reform needed to encompass all of society, along theocratic lines modelled by Old Testament Israel: there should be one covenanted community under God, Zwingli believed, in which the sword of government would be borne by the magistrates but whose use would be directed by the "prophet" (minister). It was the prophet who interpreted God's will for the covenanted community as a whole.² In other words, Zwingli envisioned the leader of the church guiding the entire unified enterprise, civil and religious, according to biblical standards. Clearly, this unitary reform vision left little room for dissent in matters of faith and conscience.

Beginning in 1518, Zwingli managed to bring about reform to the entire canton of Zurich in the space of seven years of expert preaching and exertion of influence. Although he held no seat on city council, nevertheless he exercised considerable political power in Zurich, to the point of encouraging Zurich to confront the Catholic cantons economically and militarily. The result eventually was war. The first Kappel War of 1529, in which Protestant forces vastly outnumbered the Catholic, was resolved peacefully by negotiation – much to Zwingli's disappointment. The second Kappel War of 1531 took place at Zurich's intitiative,

---

1 David Y. Neufeld expertly examines the later phases of this history in Zurich. See his recently-defended doctoral dissertation, "Marginal Coexistence: Anabaptists between Persecution and Toleration in Reformed Zurich, 1585-1650," Department of History, University of Arizona, 2018. Earlier access to this dissertation would have provided more detail and nuance to this present chapter.

2 "Zwingli looked to the kings of Israel for his polity: the king was appointed by God to rule with the sword, enforcing God's laws and ensuring true worship, but the conduit for God's will was the prophet, who had direct access to the divine will." Bruce Gordon, *The Swiss Reformation* (Manchester: Manchester University Press, 2002), 78.

*Hiding in Plain Sight*

with little support from other Protestant states, and resulted in the defeat of the Protestant cantons. Zwingli himself died on that field of battle.

In the aftermath of the disaster at Kappel, the evangelical states resolved never again to allow their "prophets" to dictate political events. In Zurich, it fell to Zwingli's successor, Heinrich Bullinger, to carry out the practical implications of Zwingli's theocratic vision – within the limits now allowed by the city's magistrates. Bullinger thoroughly embraced Zwingli's vision of a godly state informed by the prophetic voice of the church – agreeing at the time of his appointment in 1532, however, that the "prophets" would be silent on political matters; the clergy promised not to foment any political "unrest" or participate directly in the government itself.[3]

At the heart of Bullinger's understanding of the Christian society was his covenant theology, derived from Zwingli: the covenant God made with Abraham, through Moses and David, also held in the New Testament and for Christians. The pastor is the covenantal successor of the Old Testament prophet; the magistrates are the successors to the Old Testament kings. Nevertheless, Bullinger conceded that "like the Old Testament ruler, the magistrate alone had the power to establish religion and to discipline."[4] Zwingli's vision of the prophet directing church and state was now reduced to the magistrates governing both, increasingly integrating the church into state structures.

Although details vary from state to state, after the Kappel disaster in 1531 the Swiss evangelical states continued to

---

3 In Zurich's "Pfaffenbrief" of February 1532, Bullinger was elected to succeed Zwingli, and the clergy were admonished just to preach God's Word and not to meddle in political matters. The clergy agreed to this, as long as they could speak freely to moral issues in the community. "Mit dem Ergebnis zufrieden, bekundeten Bullinger und seine Kollegen ihren festen Willen zur Zusammenarbeit mit der Obrigkeit im Interesse von Frieden, Ruhe und Wohlstand." Leu and Scheidegger, *Zürcher Täufer*, 69-70; Gordon, *Swiss Reformation*, 140.

4 Urs B. Leu, "A Memorandum of Bullinger and the Clergy Regarding the Punishment of the Anabaptists (May 1535)," trans. by John D. Roth, *Mennonite Quarterly Review* 78, no. 1 (January, 2004), 116-117; Gordon, *Swiss Reformation*, 208.

promote the idea of theocratic covenant communities, and they consistently subordinated their churches to the power of the magistrates, each state at its own pace. Even in Zurich, under Heinrich Bullinger's leadership, the church lost its independent standing: the state became the final arbiter of church affairs. The process of "confessionalization" – the state's co-optation of the church and its use of the church as an agent of the state – began in earnest in Switzerland after 1531.[5]

From the start, the Anabaptists resisted any government interference in their churches. Although there were few Anabaptists and they lived primarily in villages and rural areas, they remained the most significant impediment to the establishment of religious unity and practice in the Swiss evangelical states. Anabaptism offered a grass roots reform alternative to centralized church reform "from above." They were more than just a minor irritant, to judge from the reactions of both church and state. The intriguing question is: how did this resistance manage to survive at all, in the face of so much powerful resistance?

First we have to understand the way reform occurred in the Protestant Swiss states. In all cases, beginning with Zurich, reformation occurred not in response to demands from the masses, but because of the actions of a few powerful and influential people in the urban centers of power. The city councils of Zurich, Bern, Basel, Schaffhausen and St. Gallen essentially decreed new church structures and forms of worship for their territories as a whole, urban and rural. This was reform from the top-down or from the center-out.

---

5 As noted in Leu and Scheidegger, *Zürcher Täufer*, 99. John Roth offers the following definition, after surveying the literature: "the term 'confessionalization' identifies a pattern in early modern Europe in which representatives of the territorial state sought to assert greater control over the daily lives and habits of their subjects by co-opting established forms of religious discipline (confessions, catechisms, visitations, church ordinances, etc.) and by bringing local clergy and religious practices under the authority of a central consistory." John D. Roth, "The Limits of Confessionalization: Social Discipline, the Ban and Political Resistance Among Swiss Anabaptists, 1550-1770," *Mennonite Quarterly Review* 89, no. 4 (October, 2015), 518, and n. 4.

*Hiding in Plain Sight*

The most obvious change came in the legislated removal of images and paintings of saints and the blessed Virgin – which the Reformed called "idols" – and the whitewashing of churches. The mass disappeared by mandate, replaced by a memorial Lord's Supper; priests were replaced by Reformed pastors who were mandated by city councils to preach the Gospel. Moral standards moved from being religious matters to becoming civil laws, the legislated "Morals Mandates," or *Sittenmandaten*. Moral lapses, which were now civil legal matters, were dealt with by a civil court, not by the church as such. And it was up to local pastors, appointed jointly by the church synod and city council, to promote the new church in the villages and rural territories. But the fact was that in the early going especially, able Reformed pastors were few and far between, especially in the countryside.

In terms of establishing a covenant society, Zurich led the way for the evangelical Swiss states, giving structural form to the concept: the civil and religious branches were provided with parallel institutions from the top of the governing hierarchy to the lowest reaches in the villages and rural parishes. In Zurich, the so-called *Ehegericht* (marriage court) was established in 1525 to adjudicate lay disputes; in 1526 its mandate was extended to moral issues in general. Cases that had formerly been referred to the bishop of Constance were now looked after by this civil body; it was staffed by two members of city council and two city ministers.[6] In Bern, a similar court called the *Chorgericht* was established, with stronger magisterial representation; a corresponding rural court was also put in place.[7]

---

6 Gordon, *Swiss Reformation*, 250. Gordon notes that the clerical members pronounced the majority of the decisions.

7 Gordon, *Swiss Reformation*, 255. "In each of the rural parishes of Berne a local morals court, known as the *Ehrbarkeit*, was set up on October 1529. These courts consisted of the parish minister and at least two elders from the community chosen by the bailiff. The *Ehrbarkeit* could not excommunicate, nor could it use torture; its competence was limited to admonition, fines, imprisonment to a maximum of three days, and the pillory." Ibid. Basel had a similar structure, with differences in detail. See Jecker, *Ketzer*, 55-57.

In the rural districts there were local representatives charged with the civil administration of state mandates. The head official in these districts was the *Vogt* (overseer or bailiff), who most often was a local elder appointed by the city; he was sometimes supported by an *Untervogt* (under-bailiff), as well as an appointed *Ehegaumer* (morals officer) whose task it was to oversee local compliance with the marriage and morals mandates. These appointed officials attempted to resolve disputes locally, whenever possible; they had limited ability to issue sanctions, and intractable cases would be sent up to the *Ehegericht* or the city council to resolve.[8]

This civil structure had its religious counterpart. The synod was created in 1528 and reorganized in 1532 as the highest body overseeing the Zurich clergy. The new synod constitution established that ministers would be appointed by the city magistrates (chosen from candidates nominated by the synod); the constitution established the duties and responsibilities of ministers and established the Mayor of the city and the head (*Antistes*) of the Zurich church as joint leaders of the synod and responsible for discipline. Standing at the head of this civil and religious structure was the city council and its court, where intractable cases went to be settled.

In reformed Zurich, Basel, Bern and Schaffhausen, the parish structure with its tithes and benefices remained intact; the minister and his family lived in the parish house, supported by the benefice (church living), which was provided with monies from tithes (church taxes, in effect), now collected and paid out by the city.[9] An important local church official was the church warden (*Kirchenpfleger*) who was responsible for keeping

---

8 Gordon, *Swiss Reformation*, 253-254.

9 Ibid., 253. Speaking of Zurich in 1525, Gordon writes "the mediaeval parish structures were confirmed: the parish boundaries, the rites of patronage and the payment of tithes were all retained." Bruce Gordon, "Reform of the Clergy in the Swiss Reformation," in *The Reformation of the Parishes. The Ministry and the Reformation in Town and Country*, ed. Andrew Pettegree (Manchester: Manchester University Press, 1993), 68.

church accounts pertaining to land, buildings, income, etc. In many cases the *Kirchenpfleger* and the *Ehegaumer* were the same person. The minister and the *Ehegaumer* would try to resolve local violations of marriage and morals mandates, but if they failed, the bailiff would be brought in and the matter might be taken to the highest levels in the city. Bruce Gordon has summarized the structure of the covenant community in the Swiss evangelical states after 1532 as a "confluence of secular and ecclesiastical authority."[10]

The basic legislation that needed to be monitored by ministers, morals officers and bailiffs was laid out in the "morals mandates" promulgated as civil laws by the magistrates. These mandates were renewed, expanded and continually reissued throughout the century. The *Sittenmandat* published in Bern in 1529 prohibited a long list of moral offences, such as:

> games, swearing, blasphemy, inappropriate clothing, drinking, licentiousness, marital conflict, impiety, unbelief, magic, superstition . . . dancing, child abuse, gambling, and jewellery, amongst other transgressions. . . . Every member of the community was expected to attend church regularly, bring their children forward for baptism in the parish church, and partake in the Reformed celebration of the Lord's Supper. During hours of worship it was forbidden to wander about the streets, to conduct business, to remain in the tavern or in one's bed.[11]

The *Sittenmandat* published in Zurich in 1530 contained similar prohibitions, including a specific set of prohibitions concerning the "erring sect of Anabaptists." All were to attend the state church and listen to the preachers without contradicting or insulting them, no one was to consort with the Anabaptists, attend their secret meetings or "corner sermons" or offer such

---

[10] "From the village to the city, each church official had a corresponding secular official with whom he was expected to cooperate in the maintenance of true religion, peace, and order. The disciplinary bodies, the Ehegericht and synod, were run by a mixture of church and political leaders, all under the rule of the council, which alone wielded the sword." Gordon, *Swiss Reformation*, 255.

[11] Well summarized by Gordon, *Swiss Reformation*, 256.

people help or lodging; they were not to be tolerated in the land, the mandate emphasized. In particular, all those who held sworn offices, such as bailiffs and under-bailiffs, officials, wardens, judges, morals officials and pastors, were strongly exhorted to be true to their oaths and immediately turn over known Anabaptists for judgment.[12] There was ample legislation and administrative structure in place to completely eradicate the Anabaptists as a separate church body, and that was the obvious intent.

As can be seen in the morals legislation, pastors were now expected to play a central role in policing community behavior, along with carrying out their religious duties. According to the constitution of the Zurich synod, a pastor who failed in his appointed duties would be disciplined by the synod. The considerable duties of Reformed pastors included:

> learning, the extirpation of false belief in the parish, the reading of the council's mandates from the pulpit, care of the poor, guarding against blasphemy, the upholding of the oath in the community, regular worship, the teaching of the catechism, the education of children, visiting the sick, burial of the dead, and the maintenance of a proper household.[13]

Soon added to this impressive list of duties was the requirement that pastors were to keep careful written records of births, baptisms, marriages and deaths.[14]

---

12 Emil Egli, ed., *Aktensammlung zur Geschichte der Zürcher Reformation* (Nieuwkoop: De Graaf, 1973), document 1656, 702-711; article #9 dealing with the Anabaptists is on pages 710-711. (". . . dann wir deren unverdacht sin, si ouch in unseren landen und gebieten schlechts nit lyden noch gedulden wöllend . . . " Ibid., 710). See QGTS I, #312 for the articles specifically dealing with Anabaptists. Particularly impressive is the list of local government agents admonished to carry out Zurich's orders. Addressed are: "ober- und undervögten, weiblen, pflegern, richtern, gerichten, geschwornen, egoumern und pfarrern . . . " Ibid., 710.

13 Gordon, *Swiss Reformation*, 252.

14 See, for example, the legislation from Schaffhausen in 1539: The preachers are to identify to the authorities who is not living according to the mandates re. baptism, church attendance, etc. so they can receive the appropriate punishment. They are also to keep written records of births, baptisms and marriages.

*Hiding in Plain Sight* 79

In the countryside and the villages, it was clear that the Reformed pastors were agents of the city, as well as being religious leaders. The pastors were caught in the middle of a difficult situation, needing to preach salvation to their parishioners, and to educate them in the new faith, but at the same time sworn to exhort parishioners to civil obedience, keep records for the civil authorities, and read the latest civil mandates and pronouncements from the pulpit. They also fed local information back to the civil authorities and were bound by oath to turn their parishioners over to the authorities when failures occurred.[15] Put forward as spokesmen (and supposed paragons) of righteous living, they and their families were under intense scrutiny in their parishes and did not always manage to meet expectations.

A fundamental weakness in this system was that the vast majority of the newly-minted evangelical parish preachers were still the same men who had been the local Roman Catholic priests. The data from Zurich show that of the approximately 167 clergymen in the rural parishes between 1523 and 1531, a full seventy-five per cent had been Roman Catholic clerics prior to the Reformation. Furthermore, little was done to determine the preparation or theological orientation of these newly-minted Reformed pastors. The central criterion was their willingness to swear obedience to the city council. If they did so, they were allowed to remain in their parishes, now as Reformed pastors rather than priests.[16] The historian Bruce Gordon has said that

---

See QGTS II, #176, #177, #178. "Der bucher halber, darzu die jungenn kindli, ir vatter, mutter, derselben kind götte und gotta und die een geschriben werden sölten etc., laßen min herren inen wol gefallenn, das söllichs bescheche, doch in item corpus unnd belonung etc." Ibid., #177, p. 133.

15 This "two-way usefulness" of pastors for the civil state mirrors developments in Germany: the state used pastors to disseminate mandates and information to all corners of its territory, and pastors would convey local information back to the central government. Heinz Schilling, "The Reformation and the Rise of the Early Modern State," in *Luther and the Modern State in Germany*, ed. James D. Tracy (Kirksville, MO: Sixteenth Century Journal Publishers, 1986), 28.

16 "There was no extensive examination of the clergy to determine their theo-

" . . . the Reformed churches had little control over their clergy, most of whom had little knowledge of the new faith and even less sense of how to preach."[17] In a word, the Reformed city states inherited a church structure that was populated by pastors who often lacked pastoral gifts or a profound commitment to Reformation principles; often these pastors brought with them many of the same problems they had had as priests.

Bruce Gordon's study of clerical discipline by the Zurich Synod from 1532 to 1580 brings the situation into clear relief. The synopses of 193 individual cases brought before the synod reveal drunkenness as the most common charge, along with poor education and inadequate preaching skills, unruly family situations, with some instances of adultery, failure to appear in church and the like.[18] We read of pastors like Israel Staeheli, minister in Niederurnen in the 1560s. The synod heard that "Staeheli was drinking before the services and arriving drunk. . . . The parishioners reported that he was a terrible drinker of wine and that he did not look after his own household." He was punished by being imprisoned in the tower, but then was reinstated to his church. In 1568 he was finally dismissed "on account of his wretched preaching."[19]

The village of Bülach just north of Zurich remained a stubborn Anabaptist stronghold throughout the century. The first evangelical pastor in the village was Ulrich Rollenbutz, who simply continued to occupy the same pulpit he had

---

logical orientation; if the incumbent ministers were prepared to swear an oath of obedience to the council they were permitted to remain *in situ*." Gordon, "Reform of the Clergy," 68.

17 Gordon, *Swiss Reformation*, 139.

18 See the "Prosopography" section in Bruce Gordon, *Clerical Discipline and the Rural Reformation: The Synod in Zürich, 1532-1580* (Bern: Peter Lang, 1992), 225-279. As examples, the first case listed by Gordon is Rudolf Amman, minister at Knonau, "dismissed from his parish in 1533 for adultery and polygamy." Ibid., 225. The last case in the list is Hans Jakob Zurlinden who in 1564, just after he arrived as pastor at Rüti, "was warned that he ought not to be performing the sacraments of baptism and the Eucharist in a shameful manner" (further details not given). Ibid., 279.

19 Ibid., 268.

occupied before as a Roman Catholic priest. In January, 1528 Rollenbutz wrote a detailed letter of complaint to the overseer. He reported that the local Anabaptists were saying that they were the ones preaching the Gospel and that the Reformed preachers were preaching lies. No one was coming to celebrate the Lord's Supper anymore, said the preacher, and he feared rebellion was being fomented among the common people.[20] That was Rollenbutz's side of the story. It is apparent that he faced a parish full of Anabaptists, that it was common knowledge who they were, and that the local authorities were not acting expeditiously against them.

But the record also shows that Rollenbutz was a bombastic man, already fined as a Roman Catholic priest in 1520 for swearing at and insulting his parishioners.[21] When his letter of complaint resulted in arrests in 1528, one member of his now-reformed parish in Bülach testified in court that Rollenbutz "shouts and yells in the chancel so much that even those who are not Anabaptists don't like it, and walk out of church, and have no idea what [the pastor] is saying." This parishioner, who was not an Anabaptist, concluded by saying that since the pastor didn't follow his own teaching with works, he had no interest in going to church.[22] In 1533, now occupying another parish, Rollenbutz was called before the synod to explain why his children were stealing from people in the parish.[23]

Local Anabaptist teachers, such as the illiterate Konrad Winckler, had little difficulty making headway in the Bülach

---

20 Rollenbutz's letter in QGTS I, #245, 267-269. Summarized in Gordon, "Reform of the Clergy," 74.

21 Arnold Snyder, "Konrad Winckler: An Early Swiss Anabaptist Missionary, Pastor and Martyr," *Mennonite Quarterly Review* 64, no. 4 (October, 1990), 352-361; on Rollenbutz, 358-360. Rollenbutz was moved away from the village in 1528 but continued to be in trouble with the Zurich authorities, disciplined in 1533 for leading a dissolute life and having unruly children. Ibid., 360, n. 34.

22 Ibid., 358; QGTS, I, #246, 270.

23 His defence, in essence that "kids will be kids," was rejected by the synod and he was commanded to bring order to his home. Gordon, *Clerical Discipline*, 207.

parish. One witness reported that Winckler taught that "our preachers mislead the common people and are sinners, and can bring forth no good fruit with their teaching, and are not able to preach the truth, because they have benefices."[24] It was easy to make such arguments stick when the local Reformed pastor, installed and maintained in his position by the city and supported by the hated tithe, was someone like Ulrich Rollenbutz.

Such problems persisted here and there throughout the sixteenth century. In 1602 the case of Jacob Möschlin, pastor in Kilchberg, was brought before the provincial synod in Basel. A neighboring pastor reported that Möschlin frequented the local inn daily and periodically got so drunk that he would vomit over the tables and insult all those present. Some people had composed a little song about him that was being sung here and there. He also was said to be greedy, with a loose tongue and evil ways. Many church-goers had stopped attending at Kilchberg and were attending the nearby church in Gelterkinden.[25] As Hanspeter Jecker notes, having such a preacher as representative of the official church undoubtedly helped recruit Anabaptists.[26]

In the villages and the countryside, the Anabaptists came from among the common people, lived alongside them and were integrated working members of their communities. As community "insiders," they were able to articulate local reforming aspirations and grievances (such as the unpopular payment of tithes to support city-appointed preachers), and able to exploit natural weaknesses in the early reforming system, such as sub-standard state-appointed pastors. There was also a lingering rural mistrust of the big city magistracy and the preachers the city people chose to install in the rural parishes.[27]

---

24 Ibid. QGTS, I, #281, 297.

25 Jecker, *Ketzer*, 205.

26 "Die unglaubwürdigkeit des offiziellen Kirchenvertreters mag darüber hinaus da und dort auch Sympathien für die täuferische Alternative geweckt haben." Jecker, *Ketzer*, 206. After holding several posts as a Reformed pastor, from 1588 to 1619, Möschlin was expelled from the Zurich synod. He died a soldier in Bohemia. Ibid., 205, n. 39.

27 Christian Scheidegger notes a grass-roots solidarity with Anabaptists

*Hiding in Plain Sight*

The Anabaptist grass-roots dissidents (the so-called "corner preachers") were not educated, but they put forward simple "biblical" arguments, they lived visibly devout lives, and carried out a pointed social and religious critique. The fact that Zurich captured Konrad Winckler and put him to death in 1530 did not quell the movement of dissidents in Bülach and the surrounding territory. Almost two decades later there still were Anabaptist congregations meeting regularly there.[28]

A theological and practical difference also marked the baptizing movement. From the start, the baptizers had rejected the central evangelical tenet that sinners are saved only and exclusively by their faith in Christ's sacrifice and that one's way of life did not touch salvation as such. The Anabaptists insisted that saving faith worked within individuals and would result in obedience and a Christ-like life. If such visible "obedience" was absent, the claimed faith was not truly faith. The biblical phrase they repeated insistently was one that Martin Luther detested: faith without works is dead (James 2:17). Typical Anabaptist testimonies insisted that baptism by the Spirit changed one's heart, and baptism by water marked the beginning of a new life of faith.

There is ample evidence from Swiss sources that the majority of Anabaptists in the villages and countryside did in fact lead "reformed" lives, sometimes derided as overly puritanical lives. A witness from Basel named German Bertschi, who was not himself an Anabaptist, praised the Anabaptists publicly and profusely as "pious, god-fearing people, who pray energetically,

---

throughout the sixteenth century, an abiding interest in Anabaptist teaching, and a lingering rural mistrust of the city magistracy and its preachers. "Solidarität mit den Täufern und ein gewisses Interesse an ihrer Lehre ist auf der Zürcher Landschaft bei manchen Leuten anzutreffen und ist während des ganzen 16. Jahrhunderts nie völlig verschwunden. Gleichzeitig blieb ein gewisses Misstrauen und eine gewisse Distanz gegenüber der Regierung und den Pfarrern bestehen." Leu and Scheidegger, *Zürcher Täufer*, 69.

28 See Hans Fischer's testimony from 1548, in *Later Writings*, 57-67. Clerical misconduct was still being reported in Bülach in 1568. *Cornelius Bergmann, Die Täuferbewegung im Kanton Zürich bis 1660* (Leipzig: Nachfolger, 1916), 60, n. 2.

do not curse, do no one any harm." He stated that "there are no other people who lead a finer way of life. He wishes he could be a true Anabaptist as well . . . but he is not able, because it is too difficult . . . "[29] One Leonhard Meyer, not a baptizer, declared his admiration for the way in which the Anabaptist community disciplined members when they did something wrong.[30] The Reformed pastors countered that the Anabaptists might appear to be devout, but they were hypocrites in fact. The theological charge was that the Anabaptists were trying to be saved "by their works," which was the Roman Catholic error.

Repeated complaints by Reformed pastors that the Anabaptist ethical way of life was a return to a Roman Catholic teaching of salvation by works should alert us to a significant element of Anabaptism's grass-roots appeal among the population at large. Some historians have concluded that the rural areas remained essentially Roman Catholic in piety, particularly early in the century.[31] Among such people the "pious living" of the Anabaptists hardly resonated as a terrible theological mistake deserving of punishment, but rather the opposite. If many members of the Reformed church (and even some pastors) lived much as before, with swearing, gambling, drunkenness and the like, and this church was officially tolerated and promoted by the magistrates, then this was hardly a "reformed" church in the common understanding of "reform." At the same time, it

---

[29] " . . . lobt die teufer heftig vor allen anderen leuten, das sie fromb gottsforchtig seien, beten fleissig, fluchen nicht, tuen niemand kein leit; glaube, das kein volk seie, das ein feiner leben und wandel füere. Wünscht, das er ein rechter teufer sein künt. . . . Befind sich aber, spricht er, nicht also, das ers sein künde; den es bedunke in gar zu schwer . . . " Cited in Leu and Scheidegger, *Zürcher Täufer*, 64.

[30] Cited in ibid., 64.

[31] " . . . despite the securing of the administration of the sacraments and of discipline of the clergy, the content of religious life in the rural communities remained explicitly Catholic." Gordon, *Clerical Discipline*, 16. Speaking to the wider German Reformation, R. W. Scribner estimates that "probably no more than 10 per cent of the German population ever showed an active and lasting enthusiasm for reformed ideas." R. W. Scribner, *The German Reformation* (Atlantic Highlands, NJ: Humanities Press International, 1986), 34.

made little sense among people at the grass roots that a group of subjects who lived upright, moral and devout lives (such as was actually mandated by the magistrates in the *Sittenmandaten*) would nevertheless be condemned, jailed, exiled, and persecuted. Did evangelical reform reside with the tolerated or with the persecuted?

Arguments from observed life were more effective among the "simple people" than were sophisticated theological nuances about justification and the workings of divine grace – and the argument of a devout life had the advantage of appealing to a well-understood tradition of Catholic piety at the grass roots.

The same people who refused to kill their Swiss Catholic neighbors for being Catholic had the same problem with the persecution of "good and pious people" who lived devout lives but happened to dissent with the city authorities on biblical questions of proper baptism and church discipline.[32] The first of several pressing tasks Bullinger and other Swiss Protestant reformers faced was convincing the grass roots population that they needed to turn from Catholicism to an "evangelical," biblically-based faith, but the pastors also had to convince the rural people that they needed to embrace state-sponsored reform as the proper and exclusive religious option. This meant that the rural people had to be convinced that the Anabaptists they knew, lived with, and worked with were in effect criminals and that they had a duty to identify, help apprehend and punish their Anabaptist neighbors. This proved a difficult argument. Anabaptists were able to hide in plain sight in the villages and rural areas because they were tolerated and accepted by their neighbors and often actively protected from the authorities.

The historian Martin Haas has pointed to the unique social structure of the countryside in the fifteenth and sixteenth centuries, where *Freundschaft* (friendship) networks

---

32 "In the rural countryside, especially in areas bordering on Catholic lands, there was much less antagonism towards Catholics, and certainly little desire to wage war on old neighbours." Gordon, "Reform of the Clergy," 75. Also Gordon, *Swiss Reformation*, 138.

determined primary relationships. One's *Freundschaft* included family and extended family, but also neighbors and friends with whom one had a special emotional commitment and bond, and hence primary loyalty.[33] When local civil officials (bailiffs, judges, etc.) included Anabaptists in their *Freundschaft* (as they often did) those officials faced a very real conflict.

The Solothurn records contain one spectacular example of this dynamic. Squire (*Junker*) Rudolf von Roll, bailiff of Bechburg, repeatedly failed to carry out his official duty to arrest Anabaptists because, it was alleged, he was bound by ties to his *Freundschaft*.[34] Already in March 1535 the order went out to the bailiff to arrest Hans Büri, the well-known Anabaptist.[35] The bailiff ignored the order, as is clear from the continuous missives sent from Solothurn. According to a letter sent to the neighboring bailiff of Falkenstein in October 1537, von Roll was related to the Büri family. Solothurn asked the neighboring bailiff to intervene since von Roll wouldn't act.[36] This appeal does not seem to have generated results for the magistrates, as demonstrated by the string of virtually identical orders that continued to be delivered

---

[33] A report from September, 1538 supposedly summarizes the state of Anabaptism in Bernese territory. The numbers seem to be under-reported, but the problem of local *Freundschaft* obstructing Bern's intentions is made clear. QGTS III, #824.

[34] Haas, "Berner Täufer," 17. See QGTS III, #1217, where Solothurn writes directly to the bailiff (April 22, 1537), and ibid., #1221 (October 24, 1537) where Solothurn appeals to a neighboring bailiff to ignore jurisdictions, and to arrest Anabaptists in von Roll's territory, since he has not responded to their request for action.

[35] QGTS III, #1202 (March 12, 1535).

[36] QGTS III, #1221 (October 24, 1537). Solothurn notes that von Roll had been contacted, but had done nothing (see ibid., #1217). Perhaps he did not attend to this, said the magistrates, because he was closely related to the Büri family. ("Unnd wie wir vernämmen, sol er vorgemellten Bürinen unnd den furnämsten mitt früntschaffte verwandt sin, desßhalb sollichs villicht unnderwägen beliben.")

*Hiding in Plain Sight*

to Rudolf von Roll, bailiff of Bechburg, and were studiously ignored for years on end.[37]

In the case of Hans Büri, von Roll's relative, orders for his arrest and punishment were successfully ignored for thirty-seven years. When Hans Büri died in 1572, he was an unrepentant and unpunished Anabaptist.[38] As this case demonstrates, the reach of official power was limited by the willingness of local officials to follow orders. Laws could not be enforced locally when people valued their loyalty to each other more than obedience to orders from a distant state. Local toleration could and did stymie legislated intolerance from the center.

In the Toggenburg district in 1553, a group of Anabaptists were arrested along with their leader Jakob Maler and his wife.[39] Maler and his wife were expelled, and their property was ordered to be confiscated. When Jeronimus Stalder, the overseer for Toggenburg, sent an official (Stoffel Schloiri) with wagons and horses to gather up Jakob Maler's property, the local district officer, Ammann Schmuckli, tried to stop him, saying "Stoffel, you will have to leave here with empty wagons." The sent official cited the law and his orders to confiscate, and proceeded to load a wagon and a cart full of Maler's household goods. However, he was prevented from taking the goods from a second household, he reports in his letter, by Ammann Schmuckli and the subject's brother, who maintained that the person in question had not fled the country and so was not subject to the penalty.[40]

The obstacles put up by the local district officer appear to have been related to *Freundschaft* issues. Ammann Schmuckli was related to Elß Schmucklin from Rüti, whom the records list

---

37 See the letters from the Solothurn magistrates in QGTS III, #1228; #1229 (February 4, 1538); #1230 (March 27, 15380; #1235 (March 3, 1539); #1240 (October 18, 1540); #1243 (April 29, 1541); #1244 (November 4, 1541); #1245 (February 29, 1544); #1246 (March 14, 1544); #1247 (December 15 1544); #1262 (March 23, 1558).

38 QGTS III, #1265 (March 12, 1572).

39 See Maler's testimony in Snyder, ed., *Later Writings of the Swiss Anabaptists*, 68-75.

40 QGTS II, #393, 315-16 (June 12, 1553).

as an Anabaptist; Anthon Motsch, who was the district officer for Bischwil, had a sister also identified as an Anabaptist.[41] Expedient action was not to be expected when local officials were asked to prosecute members of their *Freundschaft* and, as the Toggenburg councilors noted in December, 1553, "they have [the support of] many of the people in the territory."[42] In light of surviving evidence, it appears that the Anabaptists imprisoned in June, 1553 were treated with leniency; several conditional sentences were handed out and the prisoners released. Some of these people proved adept at evading the law.

The district officer Anthon Motsch stood surety for Othmar Raiffer's Anabaptist sister and obtained her release from prison. But she failed to change her ways (i.e., she continued as a practicing Anabaptist) and also failed to appear at subsequent hearings. As surety, Motsch was supposed to see that she complied with the law; his excuse to the court was that she was ill and could not appear. The court threatened action if he failed to bring her to the next meeting of the magistrates. At the time of the next meeting on May 11, 1554 Motsch still had not delivered, and the threats were simply repeated.[43]

Elß from Rüti also gave the Toggenburg magistrates fits. District officer Buwhoffer and a miller from Bocksberg had stood surety for her and she was released from prison. But the local morals officer noted that she refused to recant, and she was cited before the court. She did not appear, and her sureties assured the court that she – you guessed it – was ill, apparently infected with an Anabaptist flu that flared up just when court hearings were scheduled. At the May

---

41 QGTS II, #392, 314-15 (ca. June 1, 1553): List of Anabaptists in the area overseen by Ammann Schmuckli. The list identifies 29 Anabaptists. Included in the list are Elß Schmucklin in der Rüti, a possible relative of Ammann Schmuckli (p. 315, n. 5) and Adeli Motsch, sister of Anthon Motsch (p. 315, n. 7).

42 " . . . sy haben vil des volcks im lanndt." QGTS II, #398, 322 (December 12ff., 1553).

43 QGTS II, 399, 322-325; #400; 325-27 (May 11, 1554), 327. It is not clear whether Motsch actually paid the fines or not.

*Hiding in Plain Sight*  89

hearing she again failed to appear, and her sureties told the court that she was neither at home nor in the territory.[44] At the meeting of October, 1554, the cases were reviewed again. There were more threats of action, but in the end the court turned over three recalcitrant Anabaptists to their "*fründtschafft*" as sureties, with the order that they "instruct" their Anabaptist relatives and make them go to church along with other obedient subjects. If they failed in this, a capital sentence was threatened.[45] There is no record of such action ever being taken. It appears that Toggenburg officials were reluctant, or perhaps unable, to take stern action in the face of *Freundschaft* opposition. Following this concentration of imprisonments and court actions, which covered about two years, there is no further record of action in these cases.

The records show that the Bernese authorities also struggled to enforce their mandates, with local officials continually throwing sand in the gears of official policy.[46] In the summer of 1535, some three hundred Anabaptists were reported in and around Schlossrued, which at that time was in the jurisdiction of the Lenzburg bailiff. Bern was anxious to have them arrested, but it didn't happen.[47] In 1538, Anabaptists in Aarau, Zofingen, Lenzburg and Brugg were reported to be wandering about freely in taverns and public places. Bern called on local officials to prosecute and apply the appropriate legal measures.[48] In October

---

44 QGTS II, 399, 322-325; #400; 325-27 (May 11, 1554): "Die frow sige nit anhaimsch noch by land." 327.

45 In the case of Jacob Thundli and Elß uff der Rüti, "Das sollent sy och von der fründtschafft underwißen werden." QGTS II, #401, 327-329 (October 17, 1554), 328.

46 QGTS III, #198. In 1533, the "lantweibel" claimed not to be sure of the legal rights of the accused, and failed to carry out Bern's orders, for example.

47 QGTS III, #224 (June 29, 1535). Bern communicated with the Lenzburg bailiff and Catholic Luzern, urging Luzern officials to pursue Anabaptists even into Bern's territory, and promising that Bern would do likewise.

48 QGTS III, #247 (Aug. 6, 1538). Bern to Aarau, Zofingen, Lenzburg, Brugg. Officials there were advised "das ir denen nieme khein underschluff noch fry wandel, wie ander, gestatten, sonders sy ouch nach lut und sag unser ordnung straffind, dormitt söllichs vermitten werde."

and November of 1548, Bern was again corresponding with the Lenzburg bailiff, warning that the sect was growing and copied orders to officials in Zofingen, Aarau and Brugg, emphasizing that arrests should be carried out. Furthermore, in 1548 many were reported to be attending secret Anabaptist meetings and listening to Anabaptist preachers.[49] Apparently more reminders from Bern to local officials were needed, because the earlier ones had not been heeded. In January, 1550 Bern again exhorted officials in Zofingen and Aarburg to look up known Anabaptists and ask them if they would "be obedient." If so, release them; if not, arrest them and send them to Bern for trial.[50] Notice that the problem was not finding the Anabaptists, since they were well known. The fact that repeated reminders were needed from 1535 to 1550 speaks volumes about the lax levels of local enforcement. In fact, ten years later, Bern was continuing to send reminders of enforcement to officials in those same territories.[51] The Anabaptists were hiding in plain sight, able to survive because local officials and communities did not find them threatening or dangerous and tolerated their presence.

The case of Steffan Zender came before the Zurich courts in 1574. Zender was the assistant bailiff for Äsh and was arrested for having set Anabaptists free. In his defense he said, surely disingenuously, that he had never heard that Anabaptist preaching was against the magistrates' law or against "our faith."

---

49 QGTS III, #286 (October 18, 1548): Warnung vor Wiederaufleben des Täufertums. QGTS III, #288 (November 7, 1548).

50 QGTS III, #291 (January 27, 1550).

51 See #996 (May 30, 1551) for Bern's warning to officials in Burgdorf, Trachselwald, Sumißwald, Signau, Münsingen, and Hönstetten. Anabaptists in Aarburg were disputing with the preacher. Bern wanted a more detailed report about what they were saying. Those who refused to go to preaching in the state church were to be fined each time 10 pounds, and if they refused more than three times, were to be arrested. This clearly was not happening. QGTS III, #298 (October 5, 1560): Anabaptists at Arburg, Zofingen, Lenzburg. See also QGTS III, #299 (November 18, 1560): Täufer in Zofingen und Aarburg. It was reported that when Anabaptists met together and prayed, they were praying only for those of Zofingen and not for their overlords. Bern requested more information in a report.

*Hiding in Plain Sight* 91

He believed his job was just to punish vices, and the Anabaptists he released had committed none. He was released after an oath and a fine, apparently convincing the magistrates in Zurich that he had not known the extent of his duties.[52]

One way for city magistrates to break the impasse posed by reluctant officials and *Freundschaft* networks was to rely on people who were not connected to the local community. Pastors appointed by the city council were such persons. Perhaps for this reason it was usually pastors, and not local civil officials, who turned over disobedient parishioners to the city authorities for discipline – albeit usually after having attempted to correct the situation with persuasion.[53] The policing function of local clergy hardly endeared them to the grass roots, cementing their role as employees of the city state rather than as pastors concerned about their flocks.

A second more deadly way to break through the local *Freundschaft* barrier was to hire "Anabaptist hunters," who were essentially mercenaries with no kinship ties to local people. The *Täuferjäger* leave a long trail of arrests and payment-for-services in extant Bernese historical records, some earning handsome sums with the practice.[54] Perhaps it was Bern's use

---

52 STAZ EI 7-2 #125 (September 15, 1574).

53 Christian Scheidegger describes the situation in the Zurich countryside, but it seems to apply as well in Bern: "Nur selten erstatteten die niederen Beamten Anzeige. In der Rolle der Polizisten findet man fast ausschlisslich Pfarrer. Sie verzeigten, teilweise zusammen mit den Ehegaumern, die Täufer beim Rat, dem Ehegericht oder dem zuständigen Vogt." Leu and Scheidegger, *Zürcher Täufer*, 104.

54 Pauli Steinhouwern hunted Anabaptists in Signouw for 19 days and 6 nights in 1536, for which he was paid 31 pounds. QGTS III, #726, c. In July, 1536, Andres Funk was paid 2 pounds, 15 shillings for delivering Ludin Walch, Anabaptist, to Bern where he was executed. He was paid a considerable sum of money for arresting a total of 22 Anabaptists. QGTS III, #234. See Haas, "Berner Täufer," 19. There are extant lists of payments for Anabaptist arrests from the last half of 1534 on, QGTS III, #666. See also ibid., #700, #704, #713 (1535); #726, #740 (1536); #748, #756, #759, #781 (1537); #808, #838, #857 (1538); #871, #881 (1539); #897 (1540). Accounting records from the middle of 1540 to 1551 are missing. QGTS III, #897, n. 1. Fees paid to Anabaptist hunters are noted again in 1552. See #1006 (1552); #1021, #1023 (1556);

of Anabaptist hunters that put Bern in the lead among Swiss states for executions of Anabaptists, namely 49 Anabaptists put to death in the sixteenth century.[55]

Bullinger and the Swiss reformers also faced the difficult task of convincing the magistrates at the highest levels of government to act vigorously in prosecuting the religious dissenters. The city magistrates showed only sporadic interest in expending the energy necessary to eradicate the small baptizing remnant. Their interest was in maintaining peace and concord in their territories, and as long as the Anabaptists posed no obvious threat and peace remained in the countryside, there seemed little reason to stir things up by making great efforts to apprehend and punish them. The Swiss authorities often gave up trying for long periods of time. This was, if you will, *de facto* toleration, although the laws mandating intolerance remained on the books.

As one case in point, when Andreas Gut[56] and the future Anabaptist martyr Hans Landis were arrested along with others in 1589, and could not be persuaded to change their minds by the Zurich preachers, friends helped them break out of prison.

---

#1027 (1557); #1032, #1034, #1038 (1559).

55 The majority of these executions took place from 1529 to 1543. The number forty is given by Claus-Peter Clasen, *Anabaptism: A Social History, 1525-1618* (Ithica and London: Cornell University Press, 1972), 135-36. More recently, Martin Haas revised the total to thirty or thirty-two. Martin Haas, "Die Berner Täufer in ihrem Schweizerischen Umfeld I: Gesellschaft und Herrschaft," in *Die Wahrheit ist untödlich: Berner Täufer in Geschichte und Gegenwart*, eds. Rudolf Dellsperger und Hans Rudolf Lavater (Bern: Simowa Verlag, 2007), 24. Most recently, Hans Rudolf Lavater has carefully reviewed the documentation again, and placed the number at forty-nine. See Hans Rudolf Lavater, "'Was wend wir heben an . . . ' Bernische Täuferhinrichtungen 1529-1571. Eine Nachlese," *Mennonitica Helvetica* 37 (2014), 11-63, summary list, 18-19. Hanspeter Jecker notes, correctly, that the documented number of those executed does not include those who died in prison, as galley slaves, or as the result of other mistreatment. Hanspeter Jecker, "'Biss das gantze Land von disem Unkraut bereinigt sein wird.' Repression und Verfolgung des Täufertums in Bern – ein kurzer Überblick zu einigen Fakten und Hintergründen," in Dellsperger and Lavater, *Die Wahrheit ist untödlich*, 104-105.

56 For more on Gut, including his 1589 "Supplication" to the Zurich magistrates, see Snyder, *Later Writings of the Swiss Anabaptists*, 532-542.

*Hiding in Plain Sight*

They returned to their homes and lived openly and undisturbed for another 19 years before the next arrest.[57] May I repeat this number: they returned to their homes and lived undisturbed by the Zurich authorities for another 19 years. Many officials often chose to look the other way, much to the annoyance of the preachers who became the most vocal champions of a stricter application of the law against Anabaptists. It is not by accident that we read repeatedly in the Anabaptist writings from the latter half of the sixteenth century the accusation that the pastors in particular were inciting the magistrates against the baptizers. Not surprisingly, the state preachers very often took the brunt of Anabaptist criticism.

Surviving records over the next decades give an increasingly sketchy picture of actual Anabaptist presence in Swiss territories, but it appears that the lack of documentation indicates perhaps as much a lack of official interest as it does a lack of Anabaptists in Swiss lands. There are steady reports of isolated arrests, fines, and oaths of recantation in the Bernese records, for example. By 1541 the problem of perjury demanded attention: too many Anabaptists who had sworn to desist were returning to their earlier practice. Specific punishments were now mandated for the crime of perjury.[58]

The apparent benign neglect in Bernese lands changed in 1566 and was marked by the adoption of a comprehensive new Anabaptist mandate. The policy of toleration by benign neglect did have this drawback, namely that it could be revoked at any time. The new Bernese mandate is interesting in that its points of emphases reveal all the policies that had not been strictly followed or enforced and that needed to be forcefully reiterated: An oath to obey the 1534 mandate was now required of all subjects and was to be strictly applied. Attendance at church and

---

57 Leu and Scheidegger, *Zürcher Täufer*, 152. Ibid., [Barbara Bötschi-Mauz], "Täufer, Tod und Toleranz. Der Umgang der Zürcher Obrigkeit mit dem Täuferlehrer Hans Landis," 171-172.

58 See QGTS III, #932, #933, #934. An example of the new punishment for perjury – neck-irons and a public swearing of a new oath – is seen in QGTS III, #998 (December 31, 1551).

the Lord's Supper was to be strictly monitored and documented, as was the baptism of infants and marriages; no attendance at Anabaptist meetings was to be allowed. Those who disobeyed were to be exiled, with the possibility of selling their property in three months and paying a fine. Execution of backsliders was mandated again.[59] There was nothing new here, just the demand that the old laws actually be enforced.

The new hardline taken by the city resulted in two more executions: Wälti Gerber was beheaded in 1566 and Hans Haslibacher, the last Anabaptist to be put to death in Bern, was executed in 1571.[60] Their cases not only illustrate Bern's renewed commitment to eradicate Anabaptists from its territory, they also illustrate, by contrast, Bern's relatively mild policy toward Anabaptists in the 1540s and 1550s.

Wälty Gerber was a known Anabaptist in the 1530s but he disappeared from the record until he was arrested again in 1566.[61] It is worth noting that although he was described as a "leading teacher," Gerber did not interest the Bernese magistrates (or at least he is not visible in the record) for almost three decades. A similar gap appears in the record concerning Hans Haslibacher, whose martyrdom was memorialized in the "Haslibacher Lied" added to the *Ausbund* in Pennsylvania in 1622.[62] Haslibacher first appeared in the Bernese records as an Anabaptist in 1532.[63] Then there is no notice of him or his activity in the surviving documentation until 1561/1562, when he is reported to be paying a yearly fine of 100 pounds "von der töuffery wägen" (because of Anabaptism).[64] Then come notices

---

59 Jecker, "Biss das gantze Land," 104.

60 On Gerber, QGTS III, #1057; on Haslibacher, #1058ff.

61 "Bleib uff siner meinung hartneckig, besonders, das kein christ möchte ein oberer syn. Das gab im auch den todstich." Citing Johannes Haller's chronicle; official records documenting this execution are not extant. QGTS III, #1057, and note 5.

62 The song commemorating Haslibacher circulated as a print already in 1670. See QGTS III, #1063 and #1064, and notes p. 506.

63 QGTS III, #523.

64 The last of these fines is noted in 1566, after which there is a further fine in

*Hiding in Plain Sight* 95

of his arrest in 1571, ending with a report of his execution "by the sword" in October, 1571.[65] In Hans Haslibacher's case, almost forty years of "underground" Anabaptist activity lie hidden in the official record between his first arrest in 1532 and his execution in 1571.

The cases of Gerber and Haslibacher strongly suggest that the lack of official documentation must not be taken as hard, empirical evidence that there was no Anabaptist activity – only that Anabaptists remained successfully out of trouble, hidden in plain sight, probably because the authorities were happy not to have to expend resources dealing with them. In Bern, as in Zurich, the magistrates sought in vain to find a way to eradicate the baptizing movement, vacillating between "hardline" responses and milder attempts to convince by means of arguments and other inducements to conform. Systematic toleration of dissent was never considered an official option in either territory, as far as the records show, but Anabaptists who managed for decades to live hidden lives in plain sight could be forgiven for at least imagining a permanent situation in which they might be officially tolerated as law abiding religious dissidents.

A word should be said about the contention that, since Anabaptist numbers were small, they were therefore unimportant. It is true that a statistical analysis of extant court records leads to the conclusion that Anabaptism in Switzerland was adopted by only a small percentage of the population,[66] but the flip side of this observation is that Reformed attempts to

---

1569 for public disputing. QGTS III, #1058 (1561 to 1566); QGTS III, #1059 (1569,1570).

65 QGTS III, #1060 to #1062.

66 At the end of his exhaustive studies, Claus-Peter Clasen famously concluded that the Anabaptists were hardly "a powerful popular reformation movement." Claus-Peter Clasen, "The Anabaptists in South and Central Germany, Switzerland and Austria: a Statistical Study," *Mennonite Quarterly Review* 52, no. 1 (January 1978), 38. Rather than accepting that Clasen succeeded in demonstrating the irrelevance of his own work, it should be noted that institutionalized reform in Switzerland also failed to become a mass religious movement, in spite of having its hands on all the levers of power.

gain committed support for evangelical religion in the broader rural population faced the same large numbers of uninterested people. Indifference to institutionalized reform is evident in the repeated "morals mandates" that needed to be issued by Swiss authorities throughout the sixteenth century, particularly the injunctions that people were to attend sermons rather than the taverns and that they should pay attention to the preachers rather than gossiping and being openly rude.

It is worth remembering that there had been no popular ground swell for church reform among the population at large. Those few people at the grass roots who were religiously sincere and zealous for "biblical reform" were the very same persons needed in the Reformed camp, but these few people were also attracted to Anabaptism's practical piety and ethical rigor – which is what "reform" meant to most people and what the state church was attempting to impose on the whole population with its morals mandates. The Anabaptist critique was that Reformed preaching "bore no fruit" because Reformed churches were full of coerced, uncommitted members listening (or often not listening) to Reformed preachers who were state hirelings, not spiritual leaders.[67] Bullinger and the Anabaptists were pursuing committed adherents within much the same small demographic sample, and the Anabaptists had some advantages at the grass roots.

Bullinger's many-sided problem with unreformed laity, substandard ministers, and reticent magistrates provides the context for the documents translated in *Later Writings of the Swiss Anabaptists*. We can read there the Anabaptist, free church side of the argument in the ongoing battle for the hearts and minds of the small number of common folk in the Swiss countryside who actually had an ear for the reforming message.

---

67 "In both the pastoral care of the Reformed ministers and the daily lives of men and women in the parishes a residual belief in the efficacy of the power of good works and in intercession was clearly evident." So Gordon, *Swiss Reformation*, 230.

*Hiding in Plain Sight*

The huge encyclopedia of Anabaptist beliefs and teachings that was circulating in several copies in the 1580s and 90s, called the *Short Simple Confession* with no evident irony, is an example of the kind of thinking that was making its way among the simple people at the grass roots. Reviewing this document can't concern us here; those with a few days to spare can read this page-turner in Chapter 12 of *Later Writings* – over the space of 275 gripping pages.[68]

Many more stories could be told, but it is time to conclude. Anabaptist communities managed to survive in Protestant Swiss states in the sixteenth century thanks to a combination of factors, primary among which was the fact that they were tolerated and even protected in their local communities by people who knew them well. This is the form of toleration that Robert Scribner has called "the tolerance of practical rationality." What he means by this rather obscure phrase is what we have seen demonstrated in the Swiss Anabaptist story, namely "the tolerance of ordinary people, a tolerance found frequently in daily life which made little fuss about difference in belief and accepted it as a normal state of affairs." It was precisely this matter-of-fact toleration among ordinary people at the grass roots that the state church reformers had to overturn "in order to arouse awareness of confessional difference"[69] and insist that their own church had to be the only acceptable one.

Anabaptist communities also managed to survive the sixteenth century because of the diminished interest by the leading city magistrates in pursuing a policy of complete eradication. Often there simply were not enough police to enforce conformity, and the lack of local cooperation from appointed local officials simply underscored the problem.[70]

---

68 See Snyder, *Later Writings of the Swiss Anabaptists*, 170-445.

69 Bob Scribner, "Preconditions of tolerance and intolerance in sixteenth-century Germany," in Grell and Scribner, *Tolerance and Intolerance in the European Reformation*, 38.

70 Scribner lists this as the seventh form of toleration "by dint of too few resources to enforce wider conformity." This was "the de facto consequence of

In addition to the devout lives most Swiss Anabaptists lived – at the risk of arrest, exile and even execution – they also articulated an accessible biblical vision of reform that they were able to explain and defend simply and convincingly. It wasn't until the late sixteenth century and into the seventeenth that the Reformed educational effort had prepared enough pastors to reach into the villages and rural areas and successfully counter the dissident voices that the neighbours of the Anabaptists did not find threatening.

## CONCLUDING COMMENTS

The story of Anabaptist survival in sixteenth century Switzerland has reminded me of Gene Sharp's 1973 book *The Politics of Nonviolent Action*, which we discussed a lot in Peace and Conflict classes in the 1980s. Sharp made the important point that political power does not truly lay in the hands of those who stand at the centers of power but is actually dependent on the obedience and compliance of the governed. As Sharp points out, "obedience is essentially voluntary and consent can be withdrawn." Without the obedience of those standing lower down the chain of command, the commands from the center cannot and will not be carried out. The Swiss Anabaptist story is almost a case-study of Sharp's point, full of instances of intolerance being mandated by those at the center of power and being routinely sabotaged at the margins by non-cooperation, disobedience, reticence, obfuscation and other such methods.

Perhaps the Swiss Anabaptist story can help us be more mindful of what we are giving up, when we acquiesce without resistance to demands that we adopt attitudes of intolerance towards others. Incremental resistance to unjust orders is more important in giving actual shape to our world than we might imagine.

---

the powerlessness of secular authorities to enforce mandates against Anabaptism (unless recourse was had to the use of informers), so that apprehension of religious radicals relied very much on chance . . . " Ibid., 37.

A second observation has to do with the importance of community. Intolerance can be fostered only when the persons being ostracized and demonized are not intimately known by a community. Intolerance depends on fear of the unknown which allows negative stereotypes to flourish. The Swiss Anabaptist story demonstrates the power of personal relationships in countering attempts to demonize this particular group of people. Swiss people in the countryside knew very well that their Anabaptist neighbors were not Münsterites, revolutionaries, or people dangerous to society, even though the authorities repeatedly tried to depict the Anabaptists this way. The resistance in the rural communities to demonizing attempts grew directly out of personal knowledge of the people being labeled.

Perhaps those of us with an interest in discouraging the currents of intolerance that seem to be growing in our time should take a special interest in getting to know people in those groups that are being stereotyped and demonized from the centers of power. It would be interesting to see what might happen if every Mennonite family befriended one local Muslim family, for example.

The sixteenth century example of Anabaptism in Switzerland reminds us that toleration is not an ideal or abstract virtue but rather is an attitude and a way of living that is put into practice imperfectly, according to the possibilities offered by time and place. Our current time and place in the twenty-first century certainly offers many ripe opportunities for concrete acts of kindness, acceptance, and inclusion. Anabaptist descendants in North America, who now enjoy the fruits of social acceptance and economic power, should be particularly mindful of our own history as shunned outsiders who once pleaded with the powerful for toleration and inclusion. There are possibilities open to us today to befriend and welcome the marginalized if we choose to see and act.

In conclusion, I take away one central conviction from my study of toleration in the Reformation. Granted, toleration in its current social and political understanding came into being because secular leaders finally stepped in and essentially forced

Christians to stop killing one another. Nevertheless, Christians today can profitably return to the beginning of the Reformation and reconsider the calls for toleration, freedom of belief, and freedom from coercion that were initially articulated so well as central reforming principles. Christians today can and should reclaim toleration as an emphatically *Christian* virtue, rather than simply accept or reject toleration as a stance that has assumed the label of being "politically correct." Political correctness aside, Martin Luther made a central point for us as Christians when he clarified the spiritual and God-given nature of personal faith.

And finally, in keeping with Anabaptist affirmations from five hundred years ago, we can affirm that beginning from the Gospel bedrock of Christ's command that we love our neighbours and even our enemies will be the truest point of departure for people who wish to call themselves Christians. This, I believe, remains true even though it will not answer all the hard, practical questions of the specific actions of love called for in our place and time.

# J. J. (JACOB JOHANN) THIESSEN (1893-1977)

*Founded in 1978 by Canadian Mennonite Bible College, the J. J. Thiessen Lectures are named in honour of a founder and long-time chairperson of the CMBC Board. (In 2000 CMBC joined with Mennonite Brethren Bible College / Concord College and Menno Simons College to create Canadian Mennonite University.) The lectures seek to bring to the CMU community something of J. J. Thiessen's breadth of vision for the church.*

Born in Molotschna Colony in Russia, J.J. Thiessen immigrated to Canada in 1926. In 1930 he served as a mission worker in Saskatoon and later as minister of First Mennonite Church in that city. He served that congregation until his retirement in 1964. In 1917 he married Katherine Kornelsen, with whom he shared 60 years of marriage.

Throughout his life he was devoted to the cause of refugees. He was the secretary (1927-46) and later the chairperson (1946-64) of the Canadian Mennonite Board of Colonization (later the Canadian Mennonite Relief and Immigration Council). When that organization joined with other groups to form Mennonite Central Committee Canada, he served on the MCC Board. In 1948 Thiessen visited refugee camps in Europe, lobbying to bring displaced persons to Canada.

He was always active in the Conference of Mennonites in Canada. From 1943 to 1959 he held the position of moderator. He was a strong proponent of education for pastoral and lay leaders and was instrumental in establishing Canadian Mennonite Bible College (CMBC) in Winnipeg in 1947. He served as chairperson of the CMBC board of directors until 1966. In 1955 he received an honorary Doctorate of Divinity degree from Bethany Biblical Seminary.

His biography by Esther Epp-Tiessen, *J. J. Thiessen: A Leader for His Time,* was published by CMBC Publications (now CMU Press) in 2001.

## THE J. J. THIESSEN LECTURES

The J. J. Thiessen Lectures were first held in 1978 at Canadian Mennonite Bible College, Winnipeg, Manitoba, and, since 2000, have been held at Canadian Mennonite University.

1978 Marlin Miller, Professor of Theology at Goshen (Indiana) Biblical Seminary. *Mennonites and Contemporary Theology.*

1979 *Lectures cancelled.*

1980 J. Gerald Janzen, Professor of Old Testament at Christian Theological Seminary, Indianapolis, Indiana. *The Terrors of History and the Fear of the Lord.*

1981 Frank H. Epp, Professor of History at Conrad Grebel College, Waterloo Ontario. *Mennonites with the Millennium on Their Mind.*

1982 Jürgen Moltmann, Professor of Systematic Theology at the University of Tübingen, Germany. *Responsibility for the World and Christian Discipleship.*

1983 Cornelius J. Dyck, Professor of Anabaptist and Sixteenth Century Studies at Associated Mennonite Biblical Seminaries, Elkhart, Indiana. *Rethinking the Anabaptist Vision.*

1984 Kenneth Bailey, Professor of New Testament at the Near East School of Theology, Beirut, Lebanon. *Jesus Interprets His Own Cross: A Middle Eastern Cultural Approach.*

1985 Orlando Costas, Professor of Missiology at Andover Newton Theological School, Cambridge, Massachusetts.

*The J. J. Thiessen Lectures*

*The Crisis of Mission in the West and the Challenge of World Missions.*

1986 Susan Muto, Director of the Institute of Formative Spirituality at Duquesne University, Pittsburgh, Pennsylvania. *Christian Spirituality and Everyday Living: A Practical Approach to Faith Formation.*

1987 Walter Klaassen, Research Professor of Religious Studies and History at Conrad Grebel College, Waterloo, Ontario. *The Emancipated Laity: Anabaptism in Its Time.*

1988 W. Sibley Towner, Professor of Old Testament at Union Theological Seminary, Richmond, Virginia. *The Bible and Our Human Nature.*

1989 Stanley Hauerwas, Professor of Theology and Ethics at the Divinity School, Duke University, Durham, North Carolina. *Resident Aliens: The Church and Its Ministry.*

1990 Werner O. Packull, Professor of History at Conrad Grebel College, Waterloo, Ontario. *Rereading Anabaptist Beginnings.*

1991 Howard I. Marshall, Professor of New Testament at the University of Aberdeen, Scotland. *The Theological Message of the Letter to the Philippians.*

1992 George Lindbeck, Professor at Yale Divinity School, New Haven, Connecticut. *The Church as Hermeneutical Community: Jews, Christians and the Bible.*

1993 Phyllis A. Bird, Associate Professor of Old Testament Interpretation at Garret Evangelical Theological Seminary, Chicago, Illinois. *Feminism and the Bible.*

1994 David Augsburger, Professor of Pastoral Counselling at Fuller Theological Seminary, Pasadena, California. *Shepherding, Reconciling, Healing: The Church and Christian Counselling.*

1995 George Rawlyk, Professor in the Department of History, Queen's University, Kingston, Ontario. *Is Jesus Your Personal Saviour? In Search of Canadian Evangelicalism in the 1990s.*

1996 Nancey Murphy, Associate Professor of Christian Philosophy at Fuller Theological Seminary, Pasadena, California. *Christian Faith in a Scientific Age.*

1997 Richard B. Hays, Professor of New Testament at Duke Divinity School, Durham, North Carolina. *New Testament Ethics: The Story Retold.*

1998 Eugene H. Peterson, James M. Houston Professor of Spiritual Theology at Regent College, Vancouver, British Columbia. *Christ Plays in Ten Thousand Places.*

1999 T.D. Regehr, Professor Emeritus of History, University of Saskatchewan, Saskatoon, Saskatchewan. *Peace, Order and Good Government: Mennonites and Politics in Canada.*

2000 William P. Brown, Professor of Old Testament at Union Theological Seminary, Richmond, Virginia. *God and the Imagination: A Primer to Reading the Psalms in an Age of Pluralism.*

2001 Letty M. Russell, Professor of Theology, Yale Divinity School, New Haven, Connecticut. *Practicing God's Hospitality in a World of Difference.*

2002 Sean Freyne, Professor of Theology and Director of the Centre for Mediterranean and Near Eastern Studies, Trinity College, Dublin. *Jesus, Jews, and Galilee.*

2003 Paul G. Hiebert, Professor of Mission and Anthropology at Trinity Evangelical Divinity School, Deerfield, Illinois. *Doing Missional Theology.*

2004 Peter C. Erb, Professor of Religion and Culture at Wilfred Laurier University, Waterloo, Ontario. *Late Medieval Spirituality and the Sources for Peace and Reconciliation.*

2005 Paul J. Griffiths, Schmitt Professor of Catholic Studies, University of Illinois at Chicago, Illinois. *The Vice of Curiosity: An Essay on Intellectual Appetite.*

2006 Joel J. Shuman, Associate Professor and Chair of the Department of Theology, and Director for the Center for

Ethics and Public Life at King's College in Wilkes-Barre, Pennsylvania. *To Live Is to Worship: Bioethics and the Body of Christ.*

2007 Ellen Davis, Professor of Bible and Practical Theology, Duke Divinity School, Durham, North Carolina. *Live Long on the Land: Food and Farming from a Biblical Perspective.*

2008 Mark Noll, Professor of History at the University of Notre Dame, Notre Dame, Indiana. *A Yankee Looks North: Toward an Appreciation and Assessment of The History Of Christianity In Canada.*

2009 Peter Ochs, Edgar Bronfman Professor of Modern Judaic Studies, University of Virginia, Charlottesville, Virginia. *The Free Church and Israel's Covenant.*

2010 Belden Lane, Professor of Theology at Saint Louis University, Saint Louis, Missouri. *From Desert Christians to Mountain Refugees: Fierce Landscapes and Counter-Cultural Spirituality.*

2011 Peter Widdicombe, McMaster University. *Scripture and the Christian Imagination: Text, Doctrine, and Artistic Representation in the Early Church and Beyond.*

2012 Beverly Roberts Gaventa, Helen H. P. Manson Professor of New Testament Literature and Exegesis, Princeton Theological Seminary. *From Powerlessness to Praise in Paul's Letter to the Romans.*

2013 P. Travis Kroeker, Professor of Religious Studies, McMaster University. *Mennonites and Mammon: Economies of Desire in a Post-Christian World.*

2014 John Swinton, Professor and Chair in Divinity and Religious Studies, University of Aberdeen, Scotland. *Becoming Friends of Time: Disability, Timefulness and Gentle Discipleship.*

2015 Darren Dochuk, Associate Professor in the Department of History at the University of Notre Dame. *Crude*

*Awakenings: The Faith, Politics, and Crises of Oil in America's Century.*

2016 J. Richard Middleton, Professor of Biblical Worldview and Exegesis at Northeastern Seminary in Rochester, NY. *The Silence of Abraham, The Passion of Job: Explorations in the Theology of Lament.*

2017 C. Arnold Snyder, Professor Emeritus of History at the University of Waterloo in Waterloo, ON. *Faith and Toleration: A Reformation Debate Revisited.*

www.ingramcontent.com/pod-product-compliance
Lightning Source LLC
Chambersburg PA
CBHW070254100426
42743CB00011B/2241